LEGACY

*The Story of Talula Gilbert Bottoms
and Her Quilts*

LEGACY

The Story of Talula Gilbert Bottoms and Her Quilts

NANCILU B. BURDICK

RUTLEDGE HILL PRESS
Nashville, Tennesssee

Published in Nashville, Tennessee, by Rutledge Hill Press, Inc., 211 Seventh Avenue North, Nashville, Tennessee 37219. Distributed in Canada by H. B. Fenn and Company Ltd., Mississauga, Ontario.

Grateful acknowledgement is made to Sally Garoutte, editor of *Uncoverings 1984* and the American Quilt Study Group for permission to use material first published in that volume of their research papers.

Quilt photographs by Photography by Jennifer unless otherwise noted.

Maps drawn by Tanya Pitkin, based on research by Kenneth Rankin.

Design by Harriette Bateman
Typography by Bailey Typography, Nashville, Tennessee

Library of Congress Cataloging-in-Publication Data

Burdick, Nancilu B., 1917–
    Legacy: the story of Talula Gilbert Bottoms and her quilts
Nancilu B. Burdick.
        p. cm.
    Bibliography: p.
    Includes index.
    ISBN 0-934395-70-5
    1. Bottoms, Talula Gilbert, 1862-1946.   2. Bottom family.
3. Quiltmakers—Southern States—Biography.   4. Quilts—Southern
States—History—19th century.   5. Quilts—Southern States—
History—19th century.   I. Title.
NK9198.B68B87   1988
746.9'7'0924—dc19   88-11534
[B]   CIP

        3   4   5   6   7   8   9   —   95   94   93
Printed in Hong Kong through Palace Press

Contents

For Almira and Mollie Ruth:

Talula's daughters
who had the wisdom to save the records
and the quilts
that made their mother's story possible;

And for Gilbert and Mayme:

who, without realizing it,
have encouraged me enormously,
by loans of quilts,
by outright gifts,
by their hospitality,
and by simply being who they are:
my most direct living link with
my grandmother.

Preface

That hot July afternoon in 1978 when my mother opened a cedar chest in the Alabama home where I grew up and matter-of-factly lifted out a half-dozen quilts, she revealed a far different world from the one I remembered as a child. It was like being awakened suddenly from a sleep and plunged into awareness. How could it have happened that I *never really knew my grandmother?*

I had been an outdoor girl, and I remembered my grandmother as a dear, little old-fashioned woman of sweet disposition, who loved everyone, sat in a homemade chair, and serenely pieced quilts all day. I now realized how oblivious I had been to the fine workmanship and artistry in the quilts I had slept under until I went "up North" to college at age eighteen.

As my mother spread out that gorgeous array of colors and patterns on her guest-room bed, a storm of thoughts and feelings—unexpressed—overwhelmed me. Why had I not seen those beautiful quilts before? Where had they been all those years I was growing up? Why had my mother not shown them to me? In truth (it was a painful revelation), what was wrong with me that I had not *truly seen* the quilts my own children had slept under, taken away to college and worn out? My grandmother had made them, and my mother had packed them so lovingly in my cedar chest when I married a "Yankee" and left my southern home in 1940.

I had asked my mother, Almira Butler, to open that chest to look for a particular quilt. Aunt Mollie Ruth, a writer and college teacher most of her life, lay ill and dying a hundred miles away. I had gone South to see her and had spent two weeks visiting her in the hospital-annex as she sorted through her papers and talked of what she wanted done with her personal effects. She was terribly worried because several things seemed to be missing, among them the *Feather* quilt her mother had given her in 1940, "the most remarkable quilt your grandmother ever made. Someone ought to write the story of your grandmother and her quilts. Nancilu, *you* must write it," she commanded and pleaded with me to help her find the *Feather.* She was preparing to give me all her private papers, records, unpublished poems and stories—even an unfinished novel—and to leave me a small legacy of start-up money "to publish my poems, the best of my writing, or whatever you can." In fact, it seemed she was leaving me a mountain of responsibility to which I felt wholly unequal.

At that time I was a busy teacher of English and literature, loved my work, had only recently received another degree, and planned to leave shortly for England to study and travel for a month before classes began in the fall. And here was this dear aunt who had been responsible, by the beauty and accomplishments of her own life, for my having become an English teacher in the first place, telling me, "Here is something *worthwhile* for you to do!"

I had promised Aunt Mollie Ruth as I left to send her a photograph if I found the missing quilt in her sister's home; instead, I sent her pictures of six or seven stunning quilts I had photographed on a clothesline in the broiling sun of a 95° day, including the *Feather* and the *Rocky Mountain,* "Papa's favorite quilt," Aunt Mollie Ruth had said. My mother and I did not get to the bottom of even the *first* cedar chest that warm day in Alabama.

The following summer my mother, eighty-seven and gravely ill, asked her four daughters and two daughters-in-law to go upstairs and divide my grandmother's quilts among us. "Put your names on them, but do not take them now," she said.

That afternoon it fully dawned on me *my grandmother was an artist.* Though we found and divided thirty-four quilts that August day, it would be years before we realized what a skilled and productive artist she was. "Grandma" had twenty-five grandchildren, and I wondered then how many of them must still have quilts.

After my mother's death in 1980, when I inherited that unusual *Feather* quilt as well as the equally stunning *Lifeboat,* I discovered by notes attached that both had been Mollie Ruth's. They had been made just fifty years apart (1880s and 1930s). At that time I was no more than half-way through the two big boxes and several suitcases full of my aunt's papers. Busy as I was, the weight of what she had trusted me to do was overwhelming. I had a deep-seated feeling I could never accomplish the task; at the same time, torn by the suspicion something was urging me to retire from the work I loved, I had no conscious thought of doing so. I supported myself and needed the income to see my youngest son through college, but it was summer and I plunged into those containers once more—my work complicated by other boxes of old pictures and documents salvaged from the big closets I had just emptied in Almira's home.

It was then the astonishing little book turned up—resting with some old letters in a small red box where Mollie Ruth had put it—my grandmother Talula's memoir. She had written it secretly in 1943 at eighty-one. After her daughter began to doubt she would ever complete the novel she was writing about her parents' lives, Talula had written her own story and, without showing it to a soul, had put her work away in the bottom of a box of old letters and family documents. Letters subsequently found determine she gave the box to Mollie Ruth, who did not make the startling discovery until twenty-five years later. Intense correspondence with Almira soon followed. The two sisters discussed what to do with their mother's book: edit and publish it, burn it (its frankness shocked them) or most carefully decide, with their brother Burlie's help, who should inherit it. Burlie was never consulted, the decision never made, and the little book was again put away to lie hidden for twelve more years. By seeming coincidence, and without anyone's knowledge or intention (except perhaps Mollie Ruth's), it came into my hands.

I will never forget the day I discovered that handwritten, two-hundred-page book. Whatever I had begun to do was forgotten, for I was so fascinated I could not put the book down until I had read and then re-read it. Amazed and incredulous, I had a strange feeling I was discovering myself. From that day my life seemed to take on a momentum of its own, and before the next school year was over, I would (it shocks me even now to remember it) hand in my resignation at the last minute and retire. That little book and those two special quilts marked for me the beginning of a curious sensation that I was being led against my will down a strange new path. Years later a perfect stranger would come up to me and say, "Your grandmother has chosen you."

"What?" I asked, incredulous, and Michelle (for I soon learned her name) repeated it with emphasis.

"Don't you understand?" Michelle explained. "I had chills

while you were talking. Haven't *you* ever felt *your grandmother chose you* to tell her story?"

I had somewhat timidly walked up before a roomful of quilters at the Big Tree Conference "Show and Tell" in July 1985 in Geneseo, New York, to show an album of almost one hundred of Talula Bottoms's quilts, and to explain how I had come to discover them. Grandmother's *Memoir* had prompted me to visit cousins and renew acquaintances after many years of lost contact. My travels had taken me west as far as Nevada and Washington, north to Michigan, and south to Key West, Florida.

Talula's reference in her *Memoir* to her mother Holly Gilbert's *Orange Bud* quilt and her own *Orange Bud* had taken a strange hold on me. Talula had written, "I wish I did know which of our children got it, I would try to make another like it as there is not much laid work on it." My curiosity became an obsession, so irrational was my desire to find that *Orange Bud* of Talula's—or failing that, the one her mother had made. I was convinced it would be, when I found it, a match in beauty and workmanship to the *Feather* and the *Rocky Mountain*. My imagined image of that quilt was like a grail leading me on a pilgrimage of self-discovery; in getting to know my grandmother through those journeys and the 120 quilts thus far located, I have been compelled to take many risks, interpret dozens of obscure signposts, and work harder and with more self-discipline than I ever thought I could. In so doing, I have found that many of the past disasters in my life make infinite sense.

I still have not found Talula's or Holly's *Orange Bud*, but it doesn't really matter now. The rest of the story is too long and complicated to tell here. It involves coincidence after seeming coincidence, uncanny appearances—in closets at Almira's home that *had already been emptied*—of box after box of old letters; the happenstance of discovering an old quilt on exhibit in North Carolina called *Orange Bud* (not Talula's) which led to my acquaintance with and support from wonderful women long involved in quiltmaking—particularly Bets Ramsey of Chattanooga and Sally Garoutte of Mill Valley, California; the invitation to present a paper on Talula Gilbert Bottoms's quilts for the American Quilt Study Group Symposium in 1984; and finally the risk initiated by Michelle Fitch and assumed by the Kenan Quilters' Guild in Lockport, New York, of presenting an exhibit of Talula's quilts with myself as a featured speaker in 1986.

The darkest hour in my pilgrimage, six months of intense physical pain and disability, was a circumstance which proved to be a blessing. I had been in a hurry, driving on the expressway one morning in 1984, my mind on other things, as I took my two-month-old grandson to his special school when the accident happened. I lay partially paralyzed in the hospital for two weeks with a compressed spinal cord before surgery could be risked and was almost completely disabled for four months thereafter. To save my sanity, I began to piece quilts—awkwardly at first for I had to lie flat on my back. Only then did I truly begin to know my grandmother—and to sense that life had a purpose for me if I would just open my heart and slow down long enough to read the signs.

Though I have made a dozen quilts since then, piecing together Talula's story from the "scrap bag" of materials she and my grandfather, Tom Bottoms, saved has been the most complicated patchwork I ever attempted—and the most rewarding. I could never have accomplished it without the help and encouragement of innumerable people, friends, some of whom I have not even met, and the kinfolk Talula loved with all her heart.

It would take many pages just to list by name all those to whom I am indebted and to credit them properly for the ways they have assisted me. Some, but far from all, are credited in the text, captions, or notes. Here I mention most of them by groups, hoping each individual will know my gratitude is deep and lasting and that all will see reflected in the story itself the evidence of their contributions.

My own sisters, brothers, and in-laws, as well as a host of cousins, nieces, and nephews, Talula's grandchildren, and great-grandchildren, have helped by generously allowing me to examine, re-examine, and photograph their quilts, and by calling up their own memories for me. Some have taken the risk of sending their quilts great distances to be examined and photographed. Many have housed and fed me in my travels; others have taken time to write, send snapshots of their quilts, or talk on the phone about their memories of our grandmother and her quilts.

A delightful bonus has been the true southern hospitality extended by my newly found Georgia cousins, descendants of our great-grandparents, Tabitha and Matthew Gilbert, Elisa and James Bottoms. These cousins have generously opened their hearts and shared homes, meals, valuable collections,

Three *Goose Tracks* quilts span at least six decades of Talula's work and show how she used one pattern to make three entirely different quilts.

Goose Tracks I, c. 1870s–1880s. The workmanship on this unequal nine patch identifies this as an early quilt; it is entirely handmade, including the homewoven striped backing and the narrow, blind-stitched binding. The sashing strips are imperfectly matched, and the odd and uneven straight-furrow quilting show Talula still developing her quilting style and skills. The quilt was improperly stored for five years in a plastic bag and sweated badly; the cotton batting was damaged and bled through. No doubt regularly used for many years and frequently washed, it is remarkable the colors have remained so bright. The cross in center of blocks is a characteristic of many of Talula's early and later quilts.

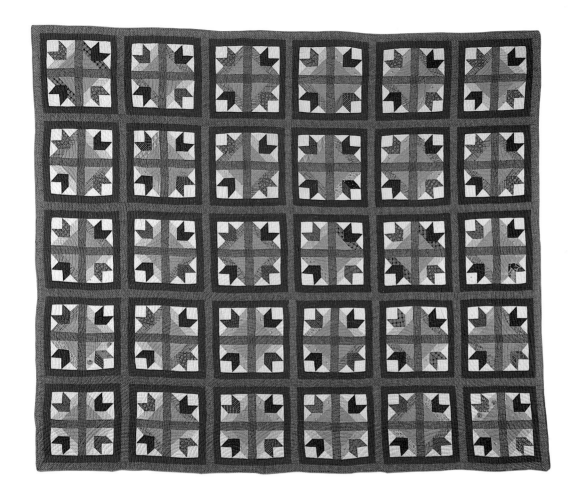

much time and conversation, and several old quilts including the *Orange Bud.* Without their help, much Civil War background and Fayette County family information would be missing from Talula's story. My acquaintance with them was made possible by the Gilbert and Bottoms genealogies written respectively by an Alabama Gilbert cousin and by my mother. Those books, always at my elbow, were at the very root of my research.

Others have contributed in important ways: members of the American Quilt Study Group and the Southern Quilt Symposium in their lectures, reports and publications, and in letters replying to my inquiries; leaders and participants in quilt conferences, workshops, guilds, and classes; groups who have asked me to talk and warmly responded to Talula's story; the family at King View Stewardship Farm, Aurora, Ontario (some of whom read my manuscript and made helpful suggestions), and its parent body the Emissary Foundation International whose extraordinary people and publications have been a steady source of

Goose Tracks II, c. late 1800s. Each of the thirty 10½-inch blocks in this well-preserved quilt uses five or more patterned or solid color cottons framed with a 1½-inch border. The blocks are then put together with 1½-inch strips of the same green print used for the wide sashing in Goose Tracks I. A scrap quilt with feed-sack backing, the quilt is entirely handmade and quilted in shells for common use everyday, though, like many of Talula's scrap and everyday quilts, it has been well-preserved.

inspiration. Two people contributed in such major ways they must be named specifically: Lenore Cymerman, later to become my daughter-in-law, who was the first to transcribe Talula's handwritten memoir, page by page with painstaking accuracy into readable type; and my good friend Sara Walling who typed and retyped my manuscript until she knew the story by heart.

Finally, much credit is due my family for their patient encouragement and love while most of my time has been devoted to this project: my daughter Sandra and her husband, my sons James and Christopher and their wives, my five grandchildren who have seen too little of me, and my devoted husband Ken, without whose thousands of miles of driving and patient help in handling quilts, much of the essential research would have been impossible. My heartfelt thanks to all of them; and to many others who, though unmentioned here, know who they are.

Acknowledgment is particularly made to the present owners of quilts who have graciously allowed them to be photographed for inclusion in Talula's story, and to those who have sent photographs so their quilts could be counted.

Eric and Deanna Avery
Margaret Avery
Donna Sue Barnhart
Lillian Talulah Bee
Deborath Susan Bottoms
George D. Bottoms
Gilbert and Mayme Bottoms
Charlotte Bowen
Sarah Evelyn Burnash
Dan and Louise Butler
Gilbert and Marguerite Butler
Jeff and Letha Butler
Leanna Butler
Marcie Butler
Mary Alice Butler

Phillip and Becky Butler
Stephen and Angie Butler
Martha Hammack
Deborah Hargett
Annalie Maynard
Bettie Pearson
Julie Anna Potts
Robert and Irene Potts
Ruth B. Potts
Beth Scott
Pauline Stell
Anna Swart
Jewel Wellborn
Mary Wentworth
Rose Marie Wilson

LEGACY

Tom and Talula in front of their Athens, Alabama, home. [Photography by George D. Bottoms II, c. 1940; enlargement was hand colored.]

CHAPTER 1

Survivors of the Storm

The time was summer 1941, the place a little country estate near Athens, Alabama, in the heart of the Tennessee Valley. Great maple trees shaded the brick-pillared veranda of a comfortable frame home set back from the road on a hundred or more green acres. Gardens and orchards, fields of cotton and corn, and a level meadow dotted with grazing cattle spread out to a woods of loblolly pines and oak saplings in the distance. A split-rail fence zigzagged across one corner and disappeared behind the weathered barn.

Driving by this pastoral scene, one might slow down to catch a glimpse of two old-fashioned people working among blossoming shrubs and luxuriant beds of flowers framing the yard. The old couple would be moving about their tasks joyfully like an aging Adam and Eve tending their garden, pausing occasionally to look with awe at the scarlet display of climbing roses trailing along a wire fence and spilling onto the ground. Or one might see them resting contentedly on the veranda in their rocking chairs.

The old woman's face would be youthful with the joy of accomplishment as she picked up her needle and cloth. Her busy hands were piecing the blocks of what was perhaps her two- or three-hundredth quilt. She had long since stopped counting them, had given most of them away, and was fast filling an old round-topped trunk with others.

The old man would be just as busy with his deep thoughts, occasional writing, and determined commitment to living out life in perfect obedience to the will of God. He had only recently published "A Communication," a leaflet defending his faith and explaining why he was not affiliated with any religious denomination.

Fayette County Courthouse, c. 1825, oldest surviving county courthouse in Georgia. It survived attempted burning by a detachment of Sherman's Cavalry in 1864 when a Yankee-hating lawyer of the town diverted their attention by displaying a large Confederate flag in his window. The Yankees took time to arrest him and put him on a mule to take him to the Union camp, thus giving Ross's Texas Cavalry time to "put them to run" and save both the lawyer and the courthouse (*The History of Fayette County*). Photo by N.B., 1986.

Within a few months the nation would be plunged into another war and Tom and Talula Bottoms would see the sacrifice of one more member of their family, their second grandson. Two major wars had already invaded the lives of these two, taking a son, mother, father, and brothers, but life was still not over for them. They would live to see this war ended, and the world left with yet another uneasy peace.

Talula had been just two years old in 1864 and Tom not quite four when the Civil War plunged with ruthless force into their native Fayette County, Georgia. When it left, the small towns and peaceful countryside were scarred and desolate. The earliest memories of those two old folks were of that war, and beneath those memories were images too terrifying to be remembered or talked about. One dark night of burning and massacre in the very heart of Fayette County had stunned its people to silence but had not killed their spirits.

The two states where Talula and Tom Bottoms lived out their lives. Their childhood homes were in Fayette County, between Fayetteville and Jonesboro, Georgia (*Gone with the Wind* country). After their marriage in 1883, they lived for fifteen years in the log cabin where Tom was born, then fifteen years near the village of Logan in Cullman County, Alabama, and finally, thirty-three years near Athens in Limestone County.

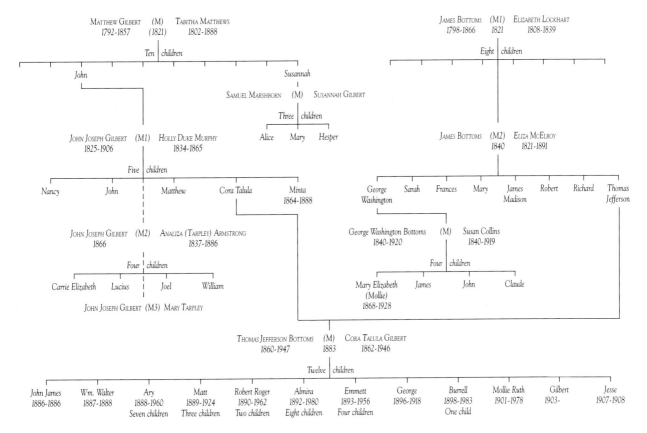

Matthew Gilbert (M) Tabitha Matthews
1792-1857 (1821) 1802-1888

Ten | children

John

Susannah

Samuel Marshborn (M) Susannah Gilbert

Three | children

Alice   Mary   Hesper

James Bottoms (M1) Elizabeth Lockhart
1798-1866   1821   1808-1839

Eight | children

John Joseph Gilbert (M1) Holly Duke Murphy
1825-1906   1834-1865

Five | children

Nancy   John   Matthew   Cora Talula   Minta
1864-1888

James Bottoms (M2) Eliza McElroy
1840   1821-1891

George   Sarah   Frances   Mary   James   Robert   Richard   Thomas
Washington   Madison   Jefferson

John Joseph Gilbert (M2) Analiza (Tarpley) Armstrong
1866   1837-1886

Four | children

Carrie Elizabeth   Lucius   Joel   William

John Joseph Gilbert (M3) Mary Tarpley

George Washington Bottoms (M) Susan Collins
1840-1920   1840-1919

Four | children

Mary Elizabeth   James   John   Claude
(Mollie)
1868-1928

Thomas Jefferson Bottoms (M) Cora Talula Gilbert
1860-1947   1883   1862-1946

Twelve | children

John James	Wm. Walter	Ary	Matt	Robert Roger	Almira	Emmett	George	Burrell	Mollie Ruth	Gilbert	Jesse
1886-1886	1887-1888	1888-1960	1889-1924	1890-1962	1892-1980	1893-1956	1896-1918	1898-1983	1901-1978	1903-	1907-1908
		Seven children	Three children	Two children	Eight children	Four children		One child			

Family tree of the Gilbert and Bottoms families.

When General Hood's Confederate army set fire to their munitions and supplies as they fled Atlanta on the night of August 31, 1864, both Talula Gilbert's and Tom Bottoms's families were among the few who had not fled Fayette County, Georgia. They remained and saw the whole northern sky enflamed by the exploding fires. Of those who survived that tragic summer and fall, some were utterly defeated, while others rose from the flames, and by their own attitudes and efforts rebuilt their homes and their lives. They are the ones who left a legacy of will and courage worth remembering.

Ordinary people who lived through those heartbreaking years were too busy gathering up the remnants of their families and trying to survive to record what they had endured. Some were utterly destitute, their suffering and need exacerbated further by the evils of the Reconstruction: exploitation, starvation, disease, and death. But they talked endlessly of that desperate time, drew courage from the oft-told miracles of survival, and their stories were overheard and remembered by their children.

Goose Tracks III. This 1930s quilt with its 15-inch blocks arranged so deceptively to look like a kind of crazy patch quilt with sashing, may have been made from Pattern No. 156 (Ladies Art Company, Quilt Patterns, 1928) found among Ruth B. Potts's collection of Talula's quilt patterns. These three *Goose Tracks* quilts show Talula's versatility in design and color, and III with its riot of pattern and color suggests a joyous and self-confident woman has come fully into her own as a person.

Among those who remembered were the children of two Fayette County families whose farms had been overrun by both Confederate and Union soldiers during the War. Although their circumstances were different, those children would later be joined in marriage: Talula Gilbert, daughter of an ambitious cotton planter who had achieved much in status and gentility before the War, and Thomas Jefferson Bottoms, sixteenth child of an unpretentious farmer and lumberman who had raised his large family in a log cabin. Their union would concentrate both

Detail of *Goose Tracks* III.

memories and many records of the two families with those two people who as children had innocently watched as the indifferent hand of war reached into their homes. Each had lost a parent and other significant family members as a result of the Civil War in Georgia, and both had been robbed of the security of an unbroken family and had missed many of the carefree joys of childhood.

Sixty years after her marriage to Tom Bottoms, nearly eighty years after the burning of Atlanta, Talula Bottoms sat at her desk in their Athens, Alabama, home. For a period of almost six months she departed now and then from her custom of piecing quilts all day, for she had decided to write down her memories of those long-ago days in Georgia. When she finished the little two-hundred-page Memoir in June of 1943, she put it away in a box of old Bottoms and Gilbert records where it was not found until twenty-five years later. What is revealed in that Memoir, in the old family documents and letters spanning more than a century, and in her legacy of more than one hundred quilts, is a woman who triumphed over the storms of war and adversity. She learned well the art of living gracefully, even joyfully, in the face of grim circumstances difficult to imagine today.

It had been Talula Gilbert's deliberate choice to marry her childhood sweetheart, Tom Bottoms. This story is largely about the circumstances, character, and accomplishments of Talula, the child, the young girl, and the woman. It is the story of her family life and the consequences of her marriage into that strong-hearted, fiercely independent, and unpretentious Bottoms family.

CHAPTER 2

The War in Fayette County

When the Civil War began in April 1861, less than a year before Talula Gilbert was born, Atlanta was only sixteen years old. Though the city was fast becoming an important inland center for trade and manufacturing, most of its streets were still unpaved, its streetcars drawn by horses. The lush countryside around the city was heavily wooded, laced with creeks and rivers, and the red earth cleared for farming, rich and productive. Long hot summers and dry weather made it especially conducive to growing cotton, and the small towns springing up around Atlanta became mercantile centers for cotton farmers. At that time most Georgia planters were small proprietors of a hundred or so acres who worked long hard hours alongside their few slaves, with whom they shared "a simple, strong and rather difficult life."[1] These men had absolute faith in the land and a kind providence to provide. The women bore many children who began very young to do their share of hard work, for few were the families who could indulge their children with many servants or the leisure to be educated to a life of "gentlemen and ladies." Both the social and spiritual life of the people centered in their churches, their business and political life around the courthouse squares in the county seats.

The John Gilbert farm was just south of Atlanta, about midway between the towns of Jonesboro and Fayetteville, less than eight miles from Lovejoy's Station. Talula Gilbert's mother was Holly Duke Murphy and her father John Joseph Gilbert. Both the Murphy and Gilbert families had migrated a generation or more earlier from the Carolinas to Georgia by covered wagon to take advantage of cheap land that could be cleared to grow cotton. The invention of the cotton gin near Savannah in 1793

Holly D. Murphy Gilbert, mother of Talula, and infant daughter Nannie, c. 1855 (*left*); Young slave woman (*right*). Pictures are copied from the original cabinet card loaned by John Lynch, great-grandson of Nannie Dickson. The two images were probably printed on the opposite sides of the card in the early 1860s by an albumen process, from tintypes made in 1855 (Anthony Bannon, Curator of Burchfield Art Center, Buffalo, New York). One is tempted to speculate that they were permanently fixed together back to back as proof the young black woman belonged to Holly Gilbert. After the tragic death of Nannie Dickson in 1924 (the infant in the picture), her daughter Leila may have sent the old cabinet card to her cousin Almira Butler. Almira had two hand-colored enlargements made and sent to Nannie's two daughters. Holly Gilbert was so profoundly affected by the War, she developed tuberculosis and died a few months after the War ended.

had made it possible for a new middle class of hard-working, ambitious people without great wealth or many slaves to own land and build substantial estates. Cotton farming was the road to success for those willing to leave a settled land and endure the hardships of frontier life. They hoped to build estates sufficient to give their children land, thereby insuring the success of their posterity.

Holly Murphy's father, John Mark Murphy, bought land in Fayette County and by the time of his daughter's marriage to John Gilbert in 1851, had succeeded well enough to give her and her new husband 207 acres near Fayetteville. The couple then worked together to build a comfortable home and to buy more land for cotton farming.

John Joseph Gilbert was the third son of Matthew and Tabitha Matthews Gilbert, pioneers who had come from North Carolina and settled in Henry County in 1821. As a young man, John began to carry mail by hack from McDonough into Fayette County. He settled there in the 1850s and became a vigorous and enterprising farmer who took advantage of every opportunity to turn a profit and acquire land. When he met and married Holly Murphy in 1851, she was the pretty young teacher at Murphy School, a rough log structure her father had built. John collected fees from parents to pay the teacher at the end of each term. Both Murphys and Gilberts were determined to give their children as good a frontier education as possible, and John Gilbert soon built a schoolhouse on his own property. He would later build another on adjoining property to serve the community; it would for a century be known as the Gilbert Schoolhouse.

Before the War started, John and Holly had three children; their cotton farm was a thriving business with its own four-horse gin. They were able to own three men and a woman, the latter apparently Holly's personal slave who may have been a gift from her father at her marriage.

John Gilbert's essential job as mail carrier exempted him from serving in the Confederate army and gave him access to the latest news from near and far. He was appointed lieutenant in the Georgia militia but was later excused from duty and assigned to a committee to look after families of departed soldiers in his district. Thus he was able to care for his own family, work his land, and devise ingenious ways of making a living in spite of war taxes and devaluation of currency. His duties were compounded by an outbreak of smallpox; in the deaths of husbands or sons at war or neighbors and family at home, he was the mainstay. He felt especially responsible for his widowed mother, Tabitha, and two widowed sisters.

When John and Holly Gilbert's fourth child and second daughter, Talula, was born on February 15, 1862, Fayette County was caught up in a fever of patriotism for the Confederate cause. The county had already contributed four full companies of young volunteers, gone "to defend their homes against invasion of a foreign foe, to protect their property from thieves and their honored and beloved women from insults and neglect."[2] Within three months after Talula's birth, two more companies in heated response to the "invasion of the Yankees into the South," volunteered to fight and joined the Confederate patriots in the Army of Northern Virginia. Talula's Uncle Sam Marshbourne resigned his position as county sheriff and organized one of those companies. "To assist in driving back the Northern vandals from our young but noble Confederacy."[3]

After the South's costly defeat a year later at Shiloh, Tennessee, the hated Yankees boldly invaded north Georgia and stole a train. The daring chase made by Southern train crews in this incident at Marietta became notorious as "The Great Locomotive Chase"; the capture and execution of the "Yankee

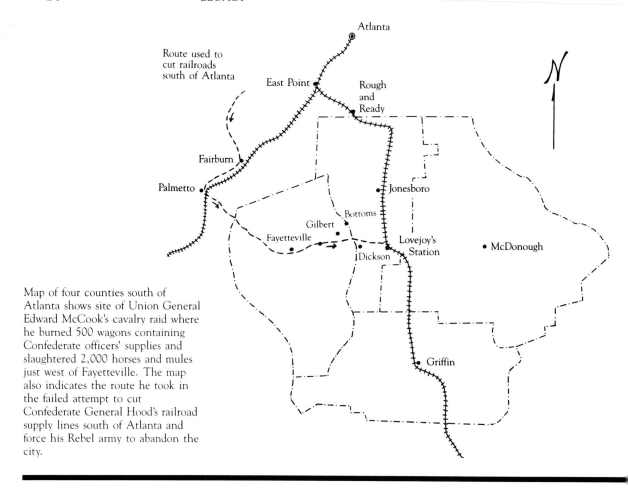

Route used to
cut railroads
south of Atlanta

N

Map of four counties south of
Atlanta shows site of Union General
Edward McCook's cavalry raid where
he burned 500 wagons containing
Confederate officers' supplies and
slaughtered 2,000 horses and mules
just west of Fayetteville. The map
also indicates the route he took in
the failed attempt to cut
Confederate General Hood's railroad
supply lines south of Atlanta and
force his Rebel army to abandon the
city.

In late July 1864 Sherman sent three cavalry divisions east and west around Atlanta to meet at Lovejoy's Station and destroy the Macon and Western Railroad. Its destruction would effectively cut the last supply line to Hood's Army of Tennessee defending Atlanta from within. Maj. Gen. Stoneman and Brig. Gen. Gerrard's divisions moved east with a total of about 5,400, but Stoneman aborted the operation by undertaking on his own an attack on Andersonville prison. He had visions of becoming a national hero by destroying the prison and rescuing all the Union prisoners there, but he and about 500 of his men were captured near Macon. Brig. Gen. Edward McCook's cavalry

division of 2,100 men was to destroy the Atlanta and Westpoint Railroad at Palmetto and Fairburn, then move on and meet Stoneman at Lovejoy's Station.

At Palmetto, McCook's raiders tore up track and burned the depot telegraph lines, one hundred bales of cotton, and other provisions; the fire could be seen twenty-five miles away. As McCook's men moved on toward Fayetteville they came unexpectedly upon the headquarters train of nearly the whole army of Atlanta loaded with officers, baggage, food, and vital military supplies. The payroll in Confederate money had been safely locked in several chests somewhere in Fayetteville.

Union Lt. Col. Horace P. Lamson (Forty-third Indiana Cavalry) wrote the following as part of his report:

". . . within four miles of Fayetteville it was ascertained that a large number of wagons laden with officers clothing, trunks, and other valuables, were corraled in different places along the road. As the column was moving quietly on, for it was yet pitch dark, details were made from the head of the column—Fourth and Second Indiana—to drop out, to take to the rear the prisoners and the best horses and mules, and kill the poorest animals with sabers, so as to avoid the noise of carbine re-

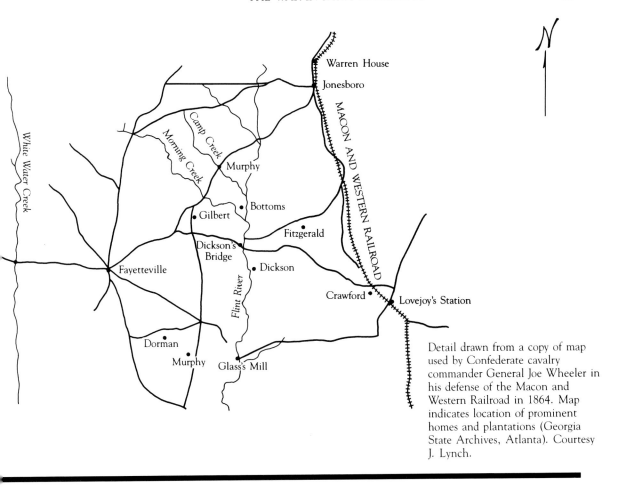

Detail drawn from a copy of map used by Confederate cavalry commander General Joe Wheeler in his defense of the Macon and Western Railroad in 1864. Map indicates location of prominent homes and plantations (Georgia State Archives, Atlanta). Courtesy J. Lynch.

ports. Not a shot was allowed to be fired. The wagons, together with the clothing, etc., was left for the rear guard, to be burnt. The number of wagons so destroyed was about 600, and between 1600 and 2000 mules were killed. At Fayetteville Second Brigade was drawn up in line at daylight. A reconnoitering party was immediately sent out who captured 130 prisoners, mostly officers, who were quartered in houses. Having arranged the prisoners—about 300—in proper place in the column, the command then moved to the Macon and Western Railroad. . . ." (Lamson's report is filed in the Official Records of the War of the Rebellion, Series I, Vol. 38, part II, page 783).

In Fayetteville, the Union cavalry also destroyed the mail, 20 boxes of tobacco, about 3,000 sacks, 4 barrels of whiskey and captured the payroll for Hood's army.

As McCook's raiders moved onto Lovejoy's Station, they were met at Flint River by Rebel pickets who were trying but failed to burn the covered bridge to keep the Yanks from crossing. McCook and his men then went on to Lovejoy's Station and tore up three miles of track, five miles of telegraph line, and burned more wagons and military supplies.

In the hot August days and nights that followed, Fayette County was truly the scene of the "most stupendous cavalry operation of the war" as "Fighting Joe" Wheeler called it. His well-trained veteran cavalry fought off McCook's raiders, repaired the railroad within three days, and captured 500–800 of McCook's men. The "war" continued an insane presence in Fayette County even after the Battle of Jonesboro. (John Lynch, "The War at Home," *Fayette County History*)

Thousands of war relics have been found and many more are still being found in Fayette and Clayton counties, mute evidence of those dark and tragic days.

robbers" gave false hopes to Georgians, no matter how violently the war had moved into their state. In little more than a year, however, news came of General Robert E. Lee's disastrous defeat at Gettysburg. After weeks of anxious waiting, John Gilbert's family learned that his sister Susannah's husband, Captain Sam Marshbourne, who had taken command of his regiment in the battle of Antietam, had survived Gettysburg. But Talula's mother, Holly, was already devastated by her father's death of a heart attack in April and the deaths of two of her brothers in the War a few months earlier. When Confederate reverses at Vicksburg, Chickamauga, and Chattanooga required recruitment of older men and young boys—leaving women and children, farms and businesses desolate—even Holly's oldest brother was taken from his wife and five small children. It seemed more than Holly could bear to lose this last brother, but the War had yet to come to the very doorsteps of the already scarred families of Fayette County.

For weeks in summer 1864 the Yankees had been moving steadily toward Atlanta with its stores of munitions and supplies, and cautious General Joe T. Johnston had frustrated their progress by his "hit-and-run" strategy. Then his victory on Kennesaw Mountain at the end of June had raised false hopes. In July, however, with Atlanta almost surrounded by Sherman's army, Confederate President Jefferson Davis grew impatient and replaced Johnston with aggressive, impetuous General John Bell Hood who had already lost a leg at Chickamauga and the use of an arm at Gettysburg. When Confederate soldiers in the field heard that Hood had replaced the much-revered Johnston as their commander, many threw down their rifles and deserted. The War in Georgia then moved into its final savage phase.

When the Battle of Atlanta on July 22 failed to rout the rebels, it was Sherman's strategy in his "Fifth Epoch of the Atlanta Campaign" to force Hood's army out of Atlanta by destroying all the city's railroad supply lines. That plan required moving aggressively west and south of the city and clashing with Confederate defenses in Fayette and Clayton counties. By that time many, many families had abandoned their homes and had fled the county to find refuge further south.

The Macon and Western Railroad ran less than eight miles from the Gilbert home. Those last days of July and the month of August were "laying-by time" in Fayette County when crops required little work and were "laid by" until they were ready for harvest in September. But no peaceful farmers hitched up their

John Joseph Gilbert (1825–1906), c. 1880s. John Gilbert's responsibilities were legion during the war years. His Civil War Record Book shows he bought raw hides of almost every conceivable animal, including dogs, had them tanned "on shares," and had a faithful slave make dozens of pairs of shoes for men, women, and children. Known as a peacemaker, he was called on so often to settle disputes, people called him "Judge" Gilbert. He became a prosperous planter and probably "bought and sold more land in the last half of the nineteenth century" than any other man in Fayette County (R. L. Guffin, *Gilbert Pioneers and Their Descendants in North Carolina and Georgia*).

wagons to take crowds of happy people to protracted meetings, however, for they suspected the whole county might soon become a battleground. Holly Gilbert kept young Nannie, Talula, Matthew, and John close, for her nerves were repeatedly shattered by the sounds of War. Almost daily an army of rifles fired within earshot so fast they "sounded like a canebrake afire," and the not-so-distant boom of cannon drove her almost to desperation. Cavalry and wagons thundered across the plank bridges and brought soldiers with sudden, rough voices to her door demanding food and provisions.

John Gilbert was torn between wanting to get his wife and children away from the ruthless intrusion of the War, and the full knowledge that if they sought refuge elsewhere, their home and farm would be destroyed. Yet he felt keenly responsible for those who remained, and it was more urgent than ever to get the mail through. As long as trains ran to Lovejoy's Station, John kept Holly, his children, and his loyal blacks on the farm to protect his property. He cared for them all as nearly like a loving father as any man could in those desperate times.

Families remaining in Fayette County witnessed the cruelty of war firsthand. Soldiers were fighting and dying in their own fields and woods; women and children fled to swamps sometimes having to fall flat on their faces to avoid the cross fire or they were driven indoors to a tenuous safety; their farms were plundered, their homes invaded by the enemy or used to shelter Confederate officers. When there was a lull in the fighting, the wounded of both sides were brought in to be fed or nursed; sometimes the women would minister to the injured where they lay wounded or dying in fields and orchards.

When a Yankee officer burst in on Holly Gilbert's family and tried to arrest a gravely wounded soldier sheltered there, ten-year-old Nannie begged the officer to leave him until, moved by the child's tears, he relented. It had been Nannie's task to wait on the helpless stranger. With unrelieved suffering and violent death so pervasive, any human life had grown more precious, the line between enemy and patriot blurred.

In a skirmish just west of Fayetteville, "a cannon ball went flying through the headboard of a bed where a farm wife was in labor." Her terrified husband ran out and pleaded for the fighting to stop until the child could be born. The Yankee commanding officer obligingly called a halt while Confederate and Union soldiers relaxed and fraternized. When all was accomplished, the officer went to the door and asked if he could see the baby, and then if he could name it. As a result of that friendly encounter, the little girl was called Shellanna Marvena—Shellanna for the shell that did not kill the mother and Marvena for the Yankee officer's wife. With baby born and named, the battle lines were again drawn and the "enemies" resumed their fighting. "Miss Anna," a great niece of that child for whom she was named, told this story again and again. Many others, bizarre or terrifying, humorous, or poignant with human kindness, are still told today by the descendants of those war-scarred families who live in Fayette County.[4]

One young Fayetteville man has dug into the *Official Records of the War of the Rebellion* to verify that indeed Fayette County was the scene of "the most stupendous cavalry operation of the war." In that midnight raid of July 28, not more than six miles from John Gilbert's farm, Union Brigadier General Edward Mc-Cook's Cavalry division of 2,500 set the night ablaze with 500 weird and pungent fires to destroy Confederate supply wagons. The wagons were loaded with officers' food and baggage thought securely hidden from the enemy. In deathly silence McCook's raiders plunged sabers into the hearts of 2,000 Confederate mules and left them bleeding to die and rot where they lay along the road. At daybreak almost every farm and village home in and around the town was raided to arrest Confederate officers lodged there for the night. It was a night of terror that so stunned people few could bear to talk about or remember it. It was agonizing for days to smell the aroma of the destroyed coffee and bacon from the burned wagons; for Fayette County had known nothing but parched corn and fatback for many months.

If families by that time had not already fled the county in wagons loaded with children and whatever belongings and live-stock they could heap on or tie behind, it was growing too late to escape.

Finally, at the end of August, the two armies clashed in the bloody battle of Jonesboro, turning the Macon and Western Railroad into a mass of twisted rails and charred ties, and At-lanta fell to the enemy. On the night of August 31, General Hood left a good part of Atlanta in flames and retreated with his army only as far as Lovejoy's Station. After an ominous lull in the fighting that had left shallow graves of soldiers and rot-ting carcasses of horses and mules strewn across Fayette and Clayton counties, there came a strange time. Except for forag-ing and an occasional skirmish, it was a quiet time. Mockingbirds stopped their singing, and buzzards swarmed over swamps and fields. Confederate and Federal soldiers fraternized with each other and made friends with local citizens and with the stream of civilians leaving Atlanta after Sherman's uncom-

Analiza Tarpley Armstrong (1837–1886) and John Joseph Gilbert, from a tintype taken sometime after their marriage in 1866. This, the only known picture of John Gilbert's second wife, shows harsh effects of post-war times in Georgia. Note Analiza's toil-worn hands and the harassed look on both faces.

Excerpts from John Gilbert's Civil War Record Book, a 5″ x 7″ leather-covered book first used in 1859 to keep Gilbert School records of children's attendance and to collect fees from parents. Geo. H. Jackson was his sister's husband and one of five "deceased" whose estates John Gilbert administered during the war.

This book contains all the affairs of Geo. H. Jackson Deces. letters ganted to J J Gilbert Dec. 2nd 1861

1861	Dec. 3	Paid tax on estate of Geo. H. Jackson	4.84	
	Dec. 11	Appraisment Bill:		
		Perishable property	481.86	
		3 Negroes	1600.00	
		lade off to widow and children support	433.00	
1863	Jan. 16	Paid to Tabitha Gilbert	114.00	
	Jan. 21	Sold 10 bushels oats		7.50
	Jan. 25	Paid for 2 bun thread	3.70	
	Feb. 27	Paid to Jas. Bottoms	28.71	
	Feb. 28	"Paid out on the Estate of Geo H Jackson more than Received by me the administrator J J Gilbert"		104.21
	Mar. 18	Received for 1½ bales cotton	8.77	
	May 5	Paid out for mending harness	3.00	
	Nov. 19	Sold one Bale cotton weighing 520 lbs. Expenses of Ginning bagging and rope (subtracted)		33.80
	Nov. 30	Sould to C C Shell in provisions to amount to in money		34.02
1864	Jan. 3	Isom & Net work 1 day	1.00	
	Mar. 10	Tax for 1864	39.52	
	"	Tax for 1863	4.67	
	"	School act. to M E Carrol	7.70	

promising order for the city to be evacuated. (A shrewd general, he had no intention of wasting time and resources on a hostile population.) That first week in September Generals Hood and Sherman met in polite conference and exchanged heated, formal letters to determine whether the War in Georgia would end. Later, Confederate President Jefferson Davis himself came to Lovejoy's Station by train and rode on horseback through Fayette County to bolster the courage of General Hood, who, after meeting with Sherman, had marched with a part of his army across the county to Palmetto.

But the War would go on. The generals so decreed after President Jefferson Davis and General Robert E. Lee refused to capitulate, though whole regiments of both sides were deserting, both civilians and soldiers beaten down with war-weariness. Most knew the Confederacy was a lost cause. Worse things than defeat were feared as they heard of Sherman's plans to bring Georgia utterly to its knees, and rumors filtered over from Alabama of his threat there to confiscate their beloved farmland itself and to populate the South with the hated Yankees.

John Gilbert and his counterparts had to contend with General Hood's ragged soldiers who, with their supplies cut off, foraged from homes and farms, captured and shot deserters, and destroyed whatever was left that might benefit the enemy. The Federal army waited, poised like an octopus—its tentacles reaching out on all sides from Atlanta a few miles to the north.

The threat of his family's starvation finally prompted John Gilbert in the midst of that sad harvest season of 1864 to take his good man, Isham, and his mule teams and make the dangerous trip south on horseback to find a place of refuge. On their return John and Isham were captured, but they knew the wooded and creek-laced terrain better than the enemy. Even as they were being taken to the Union camp, they made a daring escape through the woods and reached home safely. Then John hastily gathered up his family—with Holly expecting another child in December—and took them all, including blacks, by wagon south to Spaulding County. They stayed seven weeks, barely out of Sherman's path, and returned soon after his restless army left Atlanta in flames and began the month-long march to the sea that would leave the rich heart of Georgia a charred wasteland.

That perilous journey to a place of refuge and back home through burnt-out towns and war-scarred countryside must have affected the older children—Nannie, Bud, and Matt— even more than two-year-old Talula. Even she, however, remembered how on the way home the hungry children, black and white together, were allowed to eat bread soaked in the molasses from a broken jug that had spilled in their covered wagon, how cavalrymen had come looking for her father, how Sherman's foraging soldiers took food from their granary and smokehouse and rode off with all their sheep and hogs, and how their mother fell gravely ill after baby Minta was born and was never well again. She remembered, too, how the blacks would not leave when they were free, but stayed with the family until Holly died a year later "because they loved her." She also remembered how the good Mammy nursed both baby Minta and her own child and how the old black couple, Net and Isham, stayed on as tenants and worked the cotton fields for John Gilbert as long as they lived.

Fayette Countians heard rumors of Sherman's threat to kill "secesh" civilians, confiscate private lands, dispossess those who would resist and give possession to the hated Yankees. Sherman cited as historical precedent the dispossession of the Irish from their lands and the introduction of Englishmen and Scots during the reign of William and Mary. On Jan. 1, 1863, Gen. Sherman wrote from Vicksburg a long letter in the strongest language possible to Maj. Sawyer, Commander of the Army of Tennessee in Huntsville, Alabama. The people of Huntsville and the Tennessee Valley were prosperous cotton farmers and textile mill owners, and they fiercely resisted the Yankee invasion. Sherman had powerful supporters of his radical threat, i.e. Thaddeus Stevens and Benjamin Butler. (L. D. Miller, *History of Alabama*)

But Talula did not remember the profound shock to her mother when, only two months after Minta was born in December 1864, Holly's oldest brother came home from the War to find his plantation ruined, his wife dead, and his five children motherless.

On Christmas Eve 1865, Talula watched while her mother was put into a homemade black coffin her aunts had lined with "silk or satin." She was "troubled and ran around the room asking what they were putting my ma in that cradle for. The room was full of women; some were weeping, and one ladie took me in her arms and hurried out of the room." At the funeral Talula saw her strong father overcome with grief, but could not yet comprehend death and did not know it had robbed her of her mother.

Seven months later her father brought home a new wife, and not until then did four-year-old Talula realize her mother would never return. Her shocked sense of betrayal was compounded by her aunts' telling her to be nice because her father would bring her ma home that day: "I watched with eagerness to see my own mother, and when *she* got out of the buggy I cried." For many months afterward, Talula was inconsolable. She would go into the yard "to one certain stump that was there, and cry for a long time each day," and no one could get her to say why she was crying.[5]

Talula's new mother, Analiza (Tarpley) Armstrong, had lost her husband and infant son during the War and was so glad for the security of a home and husband she gave little thought to what her new marriage would entail. She never dreamed of the hardships she would face with five children to manage, clothe, and feed, a garden, cows, and chickens to make produce, and a house to keep according to her own exacting standards during those unbelievably harsh years after the War. Her new life required every ounce of the energy and ingenuity she possessed— and even more—for she often collapsed and went to bed with "sick headache." Then it was the child Talula's job to sit by her stepmother's bed applying an old remedy of vinegar and brown paper to relieve the pain, while Nannie, hardly into her teens, had to assume Analiza's heavy burdens. Nannie chafed in the role of servant under her stepmother's firm hand, and in a few years she would marry and leave ten-year-old Talula heir to the awesome household responsibilities. How Talula resolved her own conflicts and frustrations with Analiza was to have a life-long effect on the young girl and the woman she was to become.

When the ladies were putting her corpse in the coffin, I ran around the room asking the ladies, "What are you putting my ma in that cradle for?"

My mother had a black painted cradle made of lumber, and that resembled the lumber of outside of the homemade coffins as that was the kind in use in those old days. My father had a good carpenter to make the coffin and it was lined with silk or satten. And at the burrying I remember my Father crying and I didn't know why, as I didn't realize my mother was dead, as I was only three years old."

—Talula Bottoms, Memoir

CHAPTER 3

Broken Families

A terrifying sight, indeed, were the veteran soldiers and fifteen hundred covered wagons loaded with ammunition and supplies for the three flanks of Sherman's army searing their path through the rich heartland of Georgia. Clayton and Fayette counties were early victims of the right flank, instructed to "forage liberally off the land." Fortunate indeed were farm families like John Gilbert's, who saved their homes from burning by finding someone brave enough to live in them, while their owners sought refuge to the south.

Talula's grandmother Tabitha Gilbert refused to leave her daughter Susannah's home to save her own skin. Susannah Marshbourne had made the perilous trip to North Carolina with her three small girls to live with her husband's people and be near enough for Sam to visit from headquarters of the Army of Northern Virginia. Like a rock in the southern sun, Tabitha waited. Her brave eyes had looked starvation, wild animals, and Indians in the face; she had lived in covered wagons and log cabins and borne children in the wilderness. She would not run from an army of Yankees and leave her daughter's home to be looted and burned. Tabitha remained and watched while well-dressed, well-fed Union soldiers stripped farms of their livestock and their recent harvest, invaded homes, took clothes and jewelry, and rode off in a wild holiday mood with her own and her neighbor's livestock, food and clothes, hard-earned and sorely needed for the oncoming winter.

Younger women than Tabitha waited out the tense days of Atlanta's occupation, saw the eerie reflection of the city's burning in the night sky, and watched while Sherman's unleashed soldiers swarmed like locusts over the farms of Fayette County. One of those was Tom Bottoms's mother, Elisa Bottoms, who stayed to look after her own three small boys, her widowed daughter, Sarah, her daughter's young sons, and her aging sick

18) It surely was hard times soon after the civil war. The men that had been in war, and that were able to get back had no stock to make his crop with, for the stock had all been taken from the people at home, by the soldiers. They would kill the hogs they could find, sheep and cattle for provision for soldiers to eat, also chickens. and burst bee gums and get the honey. and burned houses, that left the women and children without homes, or provision. It was all too hard to think of. Salt got so scarce that people dug

19) dug up dirt from their smokehouses where the meat had driped, and put the dirt in an old fashion ash hopper to dry like lye for soap. They then took the water that ran thru the dirt and boiled it down to get the salt. There was no salt to put in bread or to salt fresh meat. People cooked corn pone for ever so many years without salt, and in Georgia they cook it that way until this day, as they have been trained up that way. And its good too.

An excerpt from Talula's Memoir in which she describes everyday life following the Civil War.

It surely was hard times soon after the civil war. The men that had been in war, and that were able to get back had no stock to make his crop with, for the stock had all been taken from the people at home, by the soldiers. They would kill the hogs they could find, sheep and cattle for provisions for soldiers to eat, also chickens and burst bee gums and get the honey, and burned houses, that left the women and children without homes, or provisions. It was all too hard to think of. Salt got so scarce that people dug up dirt from their smokehouses where the meat had dripped, and put the dirt in an old fashion ash hopper to dry, like lye for soap. They then took the water that ran through the dirt and boiled it down to get the salt. There was no salt to put in bread or to salt fresh meat. People cooked corn pone for ever so many years without salt, and in Georgia they cook it that way until this day, as they have been trained up that way. And it's good too.

husband, James—through it all trying to run the farm that sustained them. Sarah's husband, George Walker, had fought under "the immortal Lee" at Gettysburg, and in major battles in Virginia and Tennessee. After being furloughed home to recover from wounds, he was recalled to fight the Yankees as they invaded Fayette County and was killed. To save him from being buried in a mass grave, two brothers-in-law who had been fighting alongside him "got permission from their commanding officer, dug a little grave and buried him themselves right there in the woods" near Jonesboro.

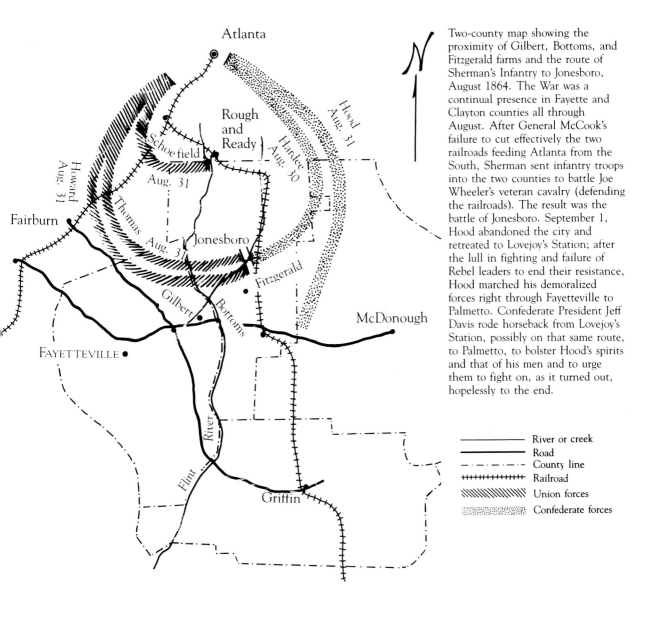

Two-county map showing the proximity of Gilbert, Bottoms, and Fitzgerald farms and the route of Sherman's Infantry to Jonesboro, August 1864. The War was a continual presence in Fayette and Clayton counties all through August. After General McCook's failure to cut effectively the two railroads feeding Atlanta from the South, Sherman sent infantry troops into the two counties to battle Joe Wheeler's veteran cavalry (defending the railroads). The result was the battle of Jonesboro. September 1, Hood abandoned the city and retreated to Lovejoy's Station; after the lull in fighting and failure of Rebel leaders to end their resistance, Hood marched his demoralized forces right through Fayetteville to Palmetto. Confederate President Jeff Davis rode horseback from Lovejoy's Station, possibly on that same route, to Palmetto, to bolster Hood's spirits and that of his men and to urge them to fight on, as it turned out, hopelessly to the end.

Susannah Gilbert Marshbourne, *left* (1843–1929). The dramatic love story of Talula's Aunt Susannah and Uncle Sam is revealed in letters they wrote just before and during the Civil War. Sam was captain of the "Fayette Planters," which he organized in 1862 to aid in "driving back the Northern vandals from our young but noble Confederacy." He achieved distinction as a courageous soldier, having fought bravely in seven major battles including Fredericksburg, Antietam, and Gettysburg. He was fatally wounded in the Battle of Cedar Creek. Susannah managed their farm while Sam was at war and raised four daughters alone during the hard years of Reconstruction. *Above right, l to r, Alice, Hesper, and Mary Marshbourne, daughters of Susannah and Samuel Marshbourne, who as little children fled Fayette County in late September 1864 with their mother and a daring "young woman dressed in men's clothes" for protection, to live in North Carolina until the War was over.*

With inflation gone wild and Confederate money almost worthless, James Bottoms, his losses compounded and over-whelmed with grief, at age sixty-five had given up, made his will, and was ready to die. His crops had been impressed for tax-in-kind to supply the Southern army or support widows and orphans; two sons and a son-in-law had already been killed in the War.

It must have pained John Gilbert in 1863 to witness James Bottoms's will, to see this trusted neighbor give up his valiant, forty-year fight to carve out a good life and build an estate for his large family in the Georgia wilderness. Just a year earlier, James Bottoms had bought a sizeable piece of wooded land from Philip Fitzgerald; James wondered if he would ever be able to pay off the $762.10 note due in December to his wealthy Irish neighbor. In a final effort to shore up his broken fortunes—to save his land and have something to leave his children—James Bottoms would sell for $1,400 in gold the child Aleck and his mother, beloved Hannah. Hannah had been his first wife's personal slave (given to Elizabeth Lockhart as a little girl by her wealthy grandfather). Hannah had been like a daughter and a sister in the Bottoms family for more than forty years. The Emancipation Proclamation signed by President Lincoln into

Camp 53d. Ga. Regt at Rapidan River   Sep 22d 1864

Dear Sue   If this reaches you it will I hope find you and the family all well. I am
well and fatter than I ever was in my life. Our trip up in the valley agreed with me
finely. I nearly lived on apples. We are now at the Rapidan River where the rail
road crosses it. We got to Culpepper day or two ago just in time to save a train of
cars. About 300 cavalry came to the rail road bridge and dastroyed it and then
made their way towards Culpepper to destroy the train that was there and we
happened accidently to march in that direction to surprise them and if we had been
20 minutes sooner would have surprised the whole force. We came very near
cutting them off. We captured 30 prisoners over 100 horses and mules and never
lost a man. I suppose as soon as the bridge is repaired we will go to Petersburg or
where ever we had started.
Sue I can not hear a word from you no way. I have not received a letter from you in
2 or 3 months. I am sorry that you are going to stay there in Ga. and get cut off
from me just to save what little we have. If you could save anything by staying it
would be an excuse but if you make ever so good a crop what the Yankees don't
destroy our folks will and what can you save by staying. I learnt that some of your
folks are persuading you to stay so you are governed by other people. Hear me.
Those that persuade you to stay are not in the war and when the Yankees come
they might not trouble them but my house will be pointed out to them as all
officers are and you will be left desolate with three little children to starve. Do you
suppose then that any of your friends that are so anxious for you to remain will
divide with you? If so and they have enough left to divide. And you wish to be cut
off where you can not see or hear from me just to remain there. I wish my children
were at my Mothers in North Carolina where they would not have to suffer for if
they stay where they are I fear they will.
Sue I want you to go to North Carolina for if you stay you will lose everything you
have to a certainty and the sooner you go the better. I think after you get entirely
cut off then you can't get away if you wished to.
You could get some soldier that is coming in here to come with you and help you
along. Mother has plenty to eat and is willing to devide with you and the children
and you would be further from the Yankees. Because your folks can't decide
against leaving is no excuse or reason why you should stay there. They can't nor
you can't shield them from the enemy. Do not come with any one except they are
sober and all right I am more than anxious to hear from you. Some few of the
company get letters accusingly though very seldom. All are well, Hiriam, George
Clasher, Roger Walker and all the rest are well.
Do not think hard of me for writing here in but I have under stood you were
persuaded to stay there and not come to North Carolina. No news. We all have
onion and green beans for dinner today which is not often
                              yours as ever
                              S   W   M

Letter from Samuel Marshbourne to
his wife Sue, September 22, 1864.

law on January first of that year would have little effect on either masters or slaves in Georgia until after the fall of Atlanta
in 1864, and to James Bottoms gold was so desperately needed
he felt compelled to let Hannah go.[1]

When in November 1864 Elisa Bottoms heard the commotion and saw the dreaded soldiers approaching, she stoically
tended her sick husband while her son, Tommie, and her
grandson, George Walker, played outside. The two little boys
in their linsey dresses caught the noisy mood of fun and frolic as
the Yankee soldiers burst beehives and beat off the stings,
rounded up mules, hogs, and chickens, and loaded their father's
wagons with animals and grain. In childish amusement they

Tabitha Matthews Gilbert (1802–1888), mother of John Gilbert and Talula's grandmother. She migrated to Georgia in 1822 as a pioneer wife and raised ten children, all of whom lived past their sixtieth birthdays. "She was a very small woman and pretty with fair complexion, black eyes, and auburn hair . . . she told me of her courtships and her marriage to my grandfather and that . . . she loved a young schoolmaster." When the older Matthew Gilbert came calling she would run and hide on top of the loom in the loom room until he went away, though he kept coming until "I guess she married him to get rid of him," Talula wrote.

The couple settled on 202½ acres of land on Little Cotton Indian Creek in Henry County, still a wilderness full of wild animals and Indians. When Tabitha had to go to the spring for water, she would "set the table leg" on her small son's dress so he would not wander. Or she would lift up a plank in the floor of the log cabin and put him in the "cellar." Her caution was understandable since she had once put him on a quilt under the trees and returned to find several Indians standing around his pallet chattering excitely. The photo first appeared in R. L. Guffin's *Gilbert Pioneers and Their Descendants on North Carolina and Georgia.*

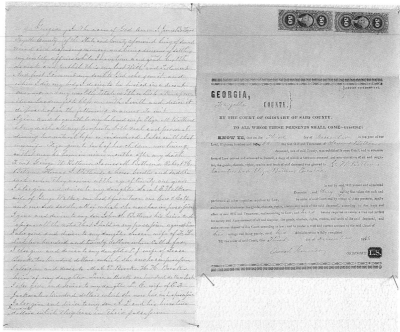

James Bottoms's will witnessed by J. J. Gilbert and others in 1863 and probated in Fayetteville in 1866, is revealing in that he could not will his children "a man apiece" as did many planters. So much of the wealth of the South resided in slaves and in cotton; by 1865 all the cotton in fields, ginyards, and warehouses had been burned, and slaves that had not been sold were free, no longer property. James had the foresight to sell his slaves in 1863, but much of the gold was already owed and what was left he gave to his grown children who sorely needed it before his death. His will states that he "gives and bequeaths" $200 (in gold) to each of his living children by his first wife Elizabeth (he had sold Hanna and Aleck for that purpose); and to all of Elisa's living sons "and any other that may be born in nine months after my death, a horse, bridle and saddle each when they reach the age of 21." To his daughters he gave "one bed and furniture, one cow and calf and one side saddle." Elisa Bottoms kept a little notebook that shows payments to most of his children were made before his death.

laughed nervously at what seemed like a strange new game, while the soldiers tried to catch the frightened chickens by hitting them with sticks and boards. The lads offered them help, and then watched uneasily, not knowing whether to laugh or cry as the Yankees rode off on their fine horses with their father's mules and the fluttering, squawking chickens, legs tied together, slung across in front of them.[2]

In December the broken families straggled back through desolate countryside, past burned out homes and ravaged land, to their own barren farms, or moved in with neighbors if their homes had been burned. Even before the war ended, they picked up the broken pieces of their lives and started over. James Bottoms brought home an old skinny mule wandering the road that "was so poor the soldiers didn't want it." That old mule was all he had to make a crop with in 1865, and Bottoms loaned it to neighbors who had none. At age 68 he was old, ill, and griefstricken, but he had remained on his farm throughout the chaos. He felt more fortunate than many farmers whose land, untended for four years, had grown up in broom straw and scrub pine, and more fortunate than those who never returned from the war, whose women and children were left to scratch out a mean living alone. Indeed, there were others who had lost much more than James Bottoms.

All across the South the brokenness of families was only a matter of degree. People like the Fitzgeralds, memorialized as the O'Haras in Margaret Mitchell's *Gone with the Wind*, had lost more than most. Their women were reduced to toil in the fields and heavy work like the rest. Philip Fitzgerald, whose plantation, Rural Home, lay just across Flint River from the Bottoms and Gilbert farms was a stocky, florid Irish immigrant. He had married a genteel Charleston woman twenty years his junior and settled in Fayette County, Georgia, as a young man in the 1830s. When the Civil War began, he owned 2,375 acres of land and 35 slaves.

Fitzgerald was Margaret Mitchell's great-grandfather, and much of the character, personality, and events of Gerald O'Hara's life portrayed in her novel came directly from the vivid stories his daughters, Margaret's great-aunts Mayme and Sis Fitzgerald, and her grandmother, Annie Stephens, told about him. It was Miss Annie Fitzgerald Stephens, who, greatly fictionalized, became the model for Scarlett O'Hara. [3]

The Fitzgerald farm, like Tara of the novel, was in the midst of bitter fighting for control of the Macon and Western Railroad that made the town of Jonesboro a battleground in late August 1864. The home itself had been saved when the spunky Miss Annie, visiting from Atlanta, went directly to Federal headquarters and demanded a guard of Union soldiers to protect it.

Like Scarlett of the novel, Annie refused to leave Atlanta, but remained there to nurse Confederate soldiers until the city fell after the battle of Jonesboro. She had taken her first-born infant back to the Fitzgerald farm through the smoldering ruins littered with dead and dying, after Atlanta had been torched by General Hood's forces. It was Miss Annie, too, who remained on the farm five miles from Jonesboro "fighting starvation and carpetbaggers until the men returned from the war." [4] But it was

Elisa McElroy (1821–1891) and James Madison Bottoms (1798–1866), parents of Thomas Jefferson Bottoms, Talula's husband. Elisa was barely nineteen when she married the forty-one-year-old James and took on the responsibilities of a stepmother to his seven living children, aged two months to fourteen years. Elisa became Talula's beloved mother-in-law and is thought to be the one who taught her the proper way to quilt. She may have helped her quilt the *Magnolia Leaf*. "She was a small woman, straight and slender. She had black, determined eyes, was quick in her movements and decisive in her manner. She was a silent and brisk sort of woman with dark hair and a quick temper. She was always straight—could set a pitcher of water on her head and walk down the road without spilling a drop," Tom Bottoms told his daughter Mollie Ruth in 1940. (Photograph first appeared in *Bottoms Families in America*.)

"The cotton crops were made by the negro slaves and one of the strange things in this eventful history is the peaceful labor of three and one-half million negro slaves whose presence in the South was the cause of the war . . . whose freedom was fought for by the Northern soldiers . . . and who made no move to rise . . . but remained patiently submissive and faithful to their owners . . . their labor produced the food for soldiers to keep fighting to keep them in slavery. . . . Here is a remarkable picture and one that discovers virtues in the Southern negroes and merit in the civilization under which they had been trained." (James Ford Rhodes, *History of the Civil War 1861–1865* [New York, Frederick Unger Pub. Co., 1961] p. 381)

"Original" house in Gone with the Wind at Jonesboro, Georgia.

Annie's sister who impressed on a young Margaret Mitchell the difference between what she called "wheat people and buckwheat people." Buckwheat people survived and rose after the storm.[5] John Gilbert was one of those buckwheat people.

Gilbert's foresight, ingenuity and industry, and just plain good luck gave him an advantage over most of his neighbors. At War's end he had lost little in terms of estate, and his record book shows he began immediately to buy and sell land, cotton, and other commodities. It shows, too, he supervised and kept records for repairing community property and rebuilding bridges burned or broken by Confederate or Yankee soldiers. But Holly's early death and the upheaval of those years had affected his family more gravely than he knew. Looking back nearly eighty years later, his daughter Talula wrote quite matter-of-factly:

> The war over and schools taken up we children went, and the teachers were mostly men, as the women had all the work of carding, spinning, weaving cloth, making clothes with their fingers, for there were no sewing machines in those days. Times were so hard in Georgia after the war.[6]

The good land, the house, and farm buildings were still there, but with food destroyed and all the cotton burned, the burdens fell heavily on John's second wife, Analiza, and his children. With almost nothing to work with and no servants to

help, women—even of genteel families—after the War had to make gardens, raise chickens, milk cows, make their own lye soap, draw water from the well to wash their clothes with no rubboards, and iron with heavy flatirons. They cooked three meals a day on open fireplaces for big families and hired men, then washed dishes and blackened pots in water brought from the well and heated in the fireplace. Such was the life that faced Nannie Gilbert when she was not yet twelve years old. Such was the life, that Talula, too, knew from early childhood, but Nannie had known another, happier time, with servants and a doting mother before the War. Talula remembered but vaguely the comfort of her mother's arms about her and the well-ordered life made easy with black help.

Although both girls found adjustment to Analiza's expectations and the stark necessity motivating her almost unbearable, their response to her was quite different. For Nannie, it was open conflict between two strong-willed people, but Talula seemed to understand what motivated Analiza and Talula's battles were fought largely within her own heart—tears and sometimes pleading the signs of her struggle. When she could, she retreated to a little haven made for herself in the loft of the milk house by the well. There her child's hands, rough and toil-worn, sewed clothes for her doll and pieced scraps together for small quilts to cover it. Her hands were awkward, and the little quilts and garments poorly sewn and ill-fitting, because no one had taught her to sew. She had accumulated the scraps, pins, and needles over weeks and months by picking up after the women who gathered from time to time with Analiza to make everyday quilts and cut and sew family clothing.

One day Talula became so engrossed in her sewing, she forgot the time. Her meticulous, quick-tempered, and over-worked stepmother flew into a rage. "She said I had to quit playing up there. She was going to have my brothers go up there and throw all my things down in the muddy lot where the stock would trample them. I began to cry and told her I wanted to save . . . [my things]. So I saved my needles and pins and quilt scraps and began to piece on a quilt."[7] After that Talula was more diligent than ever trying to please Analiza.

From this small beginning, the urge to assuage her heart-aches in creative work found early expression. Talula later resolved "to spend every moment of my time that I was not busy at something that was needed more . . . on my quilt work. . . ."[8]

My Father always had hired men to work, and a big family of his own, mostly small children for awhile. I was one of the first set of children. The women of the big families had a hard time when I was a child. They had to spin the cotton into thread and weave it into cloth, and then cut garments and make them by hand, for there were no sewing machines in those days. And the men folks had a hard time, too, for there were no farming tools except wooden beam plow stocks and scoval and other hoes to work the crops with. Everyone had to get up early in the morning and work late at nite. The women had to cook all meals on fireplace. When they boiled dinner they would hang a pot on the potrack in fireplace and boil vegatables or meat in it. Then bake bread and potatoes in oven on the big hearth at fireplace.

—Talula Bottoms, Memoir

RECEIVED *Fayetteville Ga April 30 7 1864,
of Mr. James Bottoms (33 1/2). thirty
three & one half bushels Corn*

in part payment of .... Tax in Kind.

R. W. HOGAN,
Captain and Post Q. M.

Per Lillie Blalock Banks art.

As the war years bore down on Fayette County, taxes to support the Confederate army and aid families, widows, and orphans of soldiers grew heavier by the month. It took twenty Confederate dollars to equal one gold dollar; commodities became a more practical exchange method. Some of the tax receipts saved by James Bottoms during those years are shown here.

Received $ 6 04

Of James Bottoms

For his State and County Tax for the year 1860.

FRANKLIN LANDRUM,
Tax Collector.

No........ Received..*June 3 61*.........186*4*/from

James Bottoms

100 Dollars in full to date for h   **Confederate Tax**

Specific Tax $............

General Tax ....*4 10*....

B. T. berry
County Collector.

CHAPTER 4

Wounded Women

By 1872 Analiza had given John Gilbert three more children, and Talula, at age ten, became a second mother to Bettie, Luke, and Joe. She was often kept out of school to help with the children, wash, and iron, or was required to stay up late in the evenings to finish her work. One Saturday her father came home and found her sweeping the yard while Minta and Bettie played. Talula never forgot his wordless compassion for her when he ordered the two little girls, on pain of whipping, never to let him catch Talula sweeping the yard again. It was a matter of pride for Analiza to have the big, bare, hard-clay yard swept clean for Sundays when she would bring company home for dinner from the Baptist church, or when, on alternate Sundays, John Joseph would invite some of his people from the Methodist meeting.

Those Sunday afternoons brought welcome relief to the children from the week's labors. With cousins and friends, they would play quietly up and down the steps of the high front veranda or create a world of their own under it in the cool red earth, making roads and playhouses with bits and pieces of broken crockery. Sometimes they entertained themselves under the scuppernong arbor that shaded a large corner of the back yard. One day at play the children heard strange bumping and grunting noises, and Mintie shouted her discovery that the hogs had got out of the barnyard and into the smokehouse before they were killed. This bizarre situation so tickled the children their laughter rang through the back yard while each stooped to look in at the odd sight. But the hogs, confused and frightened by the children's noise and their own plight, rushed toward the door. Mintie, in her haste to get out of the way, jumped up so fast her head struck Talula squarely in the mouth. After Talula's mouth stopped bleeding and the confusion had subsided, Analiza straightened Talula's loosened teeth the best she could, but they soon began to turn black and "were always loose after that."[1]

And in those old days, there would be a lot of the fine cotton that would stick around and up in the roof of the lint room, and my stepmother would have that saved to quilt the common everyday quilts with, tho, it would be so dusty and dirty that we'd have to put it on the bed scaffold and whip the dirt and dust out of it, then we'd have to card it into bats with an old fashioned pair of cardes then lay every bat, one by one on the lining of the quilt to be quilted, and it was already laced into the frames. and then the quilt top was put on and sewn down around edge of lining, then the everyday or nite quilts were laid off in shells to be quilted (tho the nice quilts as they called them were quilted by the piece).

—Talula Bottoms, Memoir

This run-down extension of Talula's birthplace was once the well-built room that extended from the dining room of the main house back to the old kitchen with its large stone fireplace. After John Gilbert died, this seldom-used portion was finally boarded up, and the main house rented out and neglected. John Gilbert's will left the "homeplace" to his youngest son who let it slip into hands other than the family's. It was torn down in 1985 for Oak Manor, a development of elegant homes whose occupants are doubtless unaware of the site's dramatic history. The photo was taken in 1985 after the 100-acre property changed hands.

Nannie Gilbert's marriage to John "Burke" Dickson in December 1872 required weeks of cooking for the big wedding supper after the ceremony at the Gilberts' home. A fine breakfast would follow the next morning, and then a buggy ride to the festive infare in the Dicksons' home. Dozens of breads and cakes were baked in the wide stone fireplace of the Gilberts' large kitchen, for Analiza refused to use the fine Culver Brothers stove John had just bought for her. "I'd freeze cooking on that thing thru the winter," she declared.[2]

Talula was too young to go to the infare, but she always remembered the cold wind that came up and blew Nannie's veil into a tree. The procession of buggies waited while her brother climbed the tree to retrieve it.

The wedding gave Analiza opportunity to exhibit all her skills as housewife, and, perhaps for the first time, she decided to display Holly Gilbert's beautiful quilts on all the beds. Holly had left a nice quilt for each of her five children "but one," and Nannie's quilt covered the bed in the front room for the ceremony.[3] As was the custom, Nannie and Burke would spend their wedding night there, and that quilt would be the only nice one she would have to take to her husband's fine family home where she and Burke would live for a year or more. (Time has obscured the fate of that quilt; it may have burned in the fire that destroyed the young couple's log house less than two years later.)

I have told about that old antebellum home. My Grandfather Murphy gave the farm of 207 acres to my mother. My father and mother worked together and saved some money to build that good house and to buy more land. So they planned the house, and it was convenient, with a long passage to the large kitchen that was as well built as the dwelling. The frame work was timbers mortised and pinned with wooden pegs, and both were substantially built. The kitchen was one very large room. It had my mother's loom in it fixed up so substantial and steady. The spinning wheel and the reel, and winding blades and other things needed about the threads to weave cloth were kept in that large kitchen; only the warping bars were on the outside of the kitchen, on back side, where there was a big pretty yard. . . .

Plan of house: Two very large front rooms, with a good brick chimney with good fireplace at each end of the front of house, one for each large room. Then there were three smaller rooms to the back, the two end rooms were bedrooms, the middle room was a dining room with a large closet in it. The kitchen was about 24 or 25 feet back of the dwelling with a long passage. That passage was a good wide floor with a good roof over it. The dining room was at one end of the passage, and the large kitchen was at the other end.

The furniture in the home was nice old colonial furniture. In the front rooms were beds, and the room that was not used regularly had a round center table, an old fashioned corded bed, washstand, sideboard, and two more beds after the family was larger. It also had a desk and a square table, with a drawer and a shelf about a foot from the floor; a chest and clothes table as we called it; also in later years a homemade wardrobe.

—Talula Bottoms, Memoir

Perhaps Nannie's wedding was Talula's first opportunity to see those special quilts of her mother's. Was she allowed to touch them, admire the patterns and colors, and smooth her hands across the fabric of those tangible links to her dead mother and to a past she could only vaguely remember? She was not quite eleven years old, still stealing moments above the milkhouse to sew awkwardly on her own nine-patch quilt blocks, like the one a school friend had asked her to make.

It would be many years before circumstances would allow Talula relief from her heavier duties as the only "big girl" left in the family. But she knew that someday she would find the time to make quilts like those that had so engaged her heart. She managed even then to make enough squares for her own full-sized nine-patch quilt, though they were "crank-sided . . . kindly like the first square" she had made for her friend. Her grandmother Tabitha helped her put the squares together; her stepmother quilted it for everyday, used it on the family's beds "until it was a little worn on edges." Talula would later regret her deference to her family's needs and wish she had saved her

When I was a small child, soon after the civil war, every family around where we lived in Georgia had to use lye soap for everything that soap was used for, even for bathing babies.

—Talula Bottoms, Memoir

very first quilt. But she had known the satisfaction of seeing the work of her own hands come to completion as a useful object and was familiar with every step in the process, the amount of work and the many hands that made it possible. She understood its source in the earth, from planting the cotton seed to picking, seeding, and carding the soft stuff into bats to place between the top and bottom layers, made by hand on spinning wheel and loom in the big kitchen. Even as a young girl she took seriously and for granted her essential place in providing for that large household, but she also resolved someday to make quilts simply for the love of it.

It is doubtful John Gilbert knew how cruelly the burden of work fell on Talula and, increasingly, on Minta, nearly three years younger. Eventually, both "took a bad case of rheumatism" from doing the big family wash by hand outdoors— even in winter. Analiza mixed turpentine with the "jelly soap" she made with lye to use in the hot water; the little girls rubbed and wrung out the sheets, tablecloths, and heavy, home-woven, jeans-cloth work clothes to get them clean, or lifted them in wet, heavy loads to the "battling block" and beat them, for "no washboards were known in Georgia at that time." Breathing the hot fumes of turpentine and lye soap began the disabling pain and swelling of their joints. Minta was more severely affected than Talula, and for many weeks she could not get out of bed at all. Talula remembers, "I had to crawl to the fireplace every morning when I'd get up and rub my feet and ankles until I could hobble about. Part of that time I couldn't do one thing where I had to be on my feet, so my stepmother had me card bats for quilting." Talula carded enough cotton for several quilts and so developed fully a quiltmaking skill that she would continue well into the next century.

Minta Malvina Gilbert (1864–1886), Talula's little sister. As a child Mintie took a bad case of rheumatism from doing the family wash with lye soap and turpentine. She was just a year old in 1865 when her mother Holly died of "consumption" after the Civil War.

CHAPTER 5

Healing

The hard times of the Reconstruction years were the known and ever present circumstances of Talula's childhood and youth. She remembered the ragged clothes that had to be worn through one more winter until crops could provide cotton to spin and weave cloth, until animals could be killed and their hides tanned to make shoes. She remembered the old quilts and blankets children wrapped themselves in to go to school, the corn pone day after day with no salt, the discouraging task of dripping water through the dirt and ashes from the smokehouse, to try to get a pitiful amount of salt to preserve meat so they could even kill a hog. She remembered how fish and wild game had to substitute for chicken and pork until they were sick of them. Even small children had to get up early in the morning and work hard until late at night to provide the bare essentials for the family's survival. Two incidents in particular moved her to tears: the widow left to feed a family with nothing but corn meal in the house to eat or cook, and the Negro children walking in tattered rags to their own church at Flint Ridge. She remembered, too, their fine old preacher, Uncle Berry Austin, who preached at Flint Ridge, the first one, in fact, to preach at the Gilbert Schoolhouse for the white folks when they constituted a new Corinth Baptist Church there in 1880.

Perhaps it was these harsh realities that schooled her in the self-determination and efficient use of time and energy that marked Talula's entire life. What was it, though, that enabled her to take responsibility for herself within an economic fabric that made women utterly dependent on men, and a social one that dictated so restrictively what was acceptable for their sex? Somehow, she learned early that it was her own response to people and circumstances that gave her, in some few ways, control over her own fortunes—even if that meant ignoring so-

Nancy ("Nannie") Tabitha Gilbert Dickson (1854–1924), Talula's oldest sister who was eleven in 1865 when her mother died. She "lost almost everything" when her first log home burned in 1874. This picture, made from a small tintype (c. 1870s), may have been taken in her wedding dress. "She wore a drab dress trimmed in white ruffles, a hat to match and a white veil." (Mollie Thornton, daughter of Susannah and Samuel Marshbourne, interviewed by Mollie Ruth Bottoms in 1940.) Her second home, "made of logs with a good stone fireplace," also burned several years after she lost her oldest son at age eleven and her husband at forty-three. A crumbling stone chimney and the rusted wheels of a wagon bed remain in a tangle of undergrowth to mark the spot today. Photo made from tintype loaned by John Lynch.

ciety's pretensions and not going along with her own family's expectations.

Her stepmother came from a proud, old family that had settled in Henry County to the east. Analiza's standards of perfection in housekeeping and genteel manners were a mixed blessing in those hard times. In later years Talula remembered both the terrible scenes of conflict between Analiza and her stepchildren, as well as her "sweet little voice" and generosity when she was in good humor. Within seven years Analiza had four children of her own to add to her responsibilities of cooking, washing, ironing, spinning, weaving, and clothing. Who knows what inner conflicts caused her to explode often in scenes with her stepchildren—scenes that made Talula resolve at whatever cost to avoid displeasing her.

In Talula's intense desire to please her stepmother and avoid conflict, she became a veritable slave to a family of twelve that included two live-in hired men. Rarely did she find time to slip away and piece on the blocks of another quilt she had started, and when she did her hands were cramped and calloused and often hurt so much her stitches were awkward and uneven. If she felt any bitterness about her burdensome role, she must have silently wrestled it down, though she did regret that it often required her to stay out of school.

When Talula was twelve, there were three little half brothers to tend; Joe, the middle boy, seemed always sad and hungry. Perhaps his need was for love and attention more than for food, for he took up so readily with the vagrant Joe Chambers when Chambers came begging. Little Joe would sit on the back door-step and cry, "Lule, give me some bread"; and Talula recalls that when she was through with her work, "I would take him out to the beegums [beehives], sit on the end of the bench, and sing at the top of my voice" to comfort him. Perhaps in doing so she was learning how to sing and sew her way past dwelling on the griefs and hardships of her own circumstances.

It had been in the fall of 1874, just ten years after Atlanta's burning when little Joe Gilbert was just two, that John Gilbert's household was disturbed in the middle of the night by loud knocking and frantic voices crying for help. The whole family was awakened to find Burke Dickson, scorched and breathless, asking shelter for Nannie, whose beautiful hair was dishevelled and burned to the scalp. The eastern sky, ominously aglow, told the story of their futile efforts to save their home, even before they could get the words out.

Nannie Gilbert and Burke Dickson had been married less than two years and only recently had moved into their own log house with its large stone fireplace for heating and cooking. The fire had started mysteriously in the middle of the night; Burke raced out to the well and pulled frantically on the old bucket, but with too much haste and too much strength, he tore the rope loose and the bucket plunged uselessly to the bottom of the well. Then the nearest source of water lay across the field at the new Gilbert Schoolhouse. Running there, Burke passed the old Murphy schoolhouse and saw Joe Chambers "standing on the rostrum (sic) laughing."

Returning with bucket and rope from the schoolhouse well, Burke found the fire out of control, Nannie dashing in and out to retrieve what she could. Seeing it was futile to try to save the house, Burke began to help Nannie. As he tried to pull their good front-room bed to the doorway, the headboard came off and was left to burn. Nannie's hair was singed off the top of her head, and she barely escaped the falling timbers when she made

John Marshall (Burke) Dickson (1848–1891). Listed as a soldier in the Civil War at sixteen, his marriage to Nannie Gilbert in 1874 was celebrated with elaborate festivities known as the infare. Burke was descended from an old and distinguished Georgia family. His grandfather David Dickson, a major in the Revolutionary War, later became a state senator and large landowner in Fayette County. Some of his land was bought in 1853 by Phillip Fitzgerald, and it was there he built "Rural Home," the rather plain, two-story house thought to be Margaret Mitchell's model for Tara in *Gone with the Wind.* Burke was killed in 1891 under the wheels of his own wagon loaded with logs coming from his sawmill on the Bottoms farm, leaving Nannie with four young children and pregnant with another. Photo made from tintype loaned by John Lynch.

one last dash inside to get their treasured clock. Then the two watched helplessly while their house fell in flames.

Talula remembers:

> They had a bale of seed cotton in a shed room and it got burned up too. I was just a small girl at the time and it made a terrible impression on me. . . .
>
> Joe was all right I think until he was grown. He came from a good, highstanding family. His father had a nice home and farm.
>
> . . . he told my father that he'd been all right if they had let him have the old home place of his father's and if Miss Mayme Fitzgerald had married him . . . He would not live with any of his folks after his parents died.

Burke thought Joe set fire to their house because Nannie "couldn't let him have a pot to cook his game in."[1]

Joe Chambers was a bitter, defeated man who after the Civil War lived like an animal in the woods around Fayetteville and Jonesboro. At night he would find shelter in schoolhouses. He lived off wild fruits and berries, killed squirrels and rabbits, and sometimes borrowed a good fireplace pot from Nannie Dickson. He had a little bucket he would bring to people's houses for food when he was desperate for a good meal or human contact. Bearded, shaggy, and dirty, he often went to John Gilbert's back gate. While his bucket was being filled, he would call out to Talula's little brother, Joe, who would come running. Chambers would pick up little Joe and hug and kiss him, then, taking his bucket, disappear through the orchard and into the woods.

Burke and Nannie lost almost everything, but neighbors were generous and gave what they could. John Gilbert helped by letting his daughter and her husband move into the new schoolhouse to live until they could build a new log home. Nannie Gilbert had been just ten years old, Burke Dickson only sixteen and a soldier himself, when the Civil War raged through Fayette and Clayton counties and Atlanta was consumed in flames. Tragedy stalked them through the years, and Talula's heart was often burdened by her sister's suffering and loss.

As she grew into young womanhood. Talula looked forward to her sixteenth birthday, for then she could have her ears pierced and dress up for a trip to Jonesboro with her father. Sometime that year she would have her picture made to show at family gatherings. The itinerant photographer's railroad car would be parked on the siding in Jonesboro for several weeks until farm families could save enough money to have their pictures taken.

Talula Bottoms (1862–1946), age 16. Copies made from c. 1878 tintype.

At Christmas it was customary for Tabitha Gilbert's large family to gather at her son John's house for a reunion that would spill out into the big back yard. With ten children all married and fifty living grandchildren, Tabitha and her family could no longer fit inside anyone's house. Big tables were set under the trees, for every family would bring great dishes of favorite foods. The feasting, piano playing, singing, and catching up on family news would last all day.

In 1878 many of them and Grandmother Tabitha herself would pass around little paper or cardboard-framed tintypes for all to admire. At seventy-six, Tabitha had seen sixty grandchildren enter the world—the oldest then thirty-four and the youngest aged two—and several great-grandchildren. Eight or ten of her granddaughters were of an age to begin thinking of marriage, and they would gather in groups to talk excitedly of beaux.

Talula had grown into a beautiful young woman and was already being noticed, though she was not allowed to accept the attentions of young men. Analiza had taught her to be modest and ladylike, not to raise her voice or laugh out loud, and to walk with small dainty steps. Never must she show her ankles above her shoe tops or in any way call attention to herself; she had learned to talk softly and laugh silently, always with lips closed for some of her teeth were badly decayed from that back yard incident when she was a child.

One night early in her sixteenth year, Talula awoke to find one of her front teeth had fallen out. Then the fear of going toothless into a life of spinsterhood that must have been lurking for years stunned and overwhelmed her. She began to cry and call for her father. When she "waked Pa and told him . . . he said never mind . . . that he would take me to Atlanta to get some new teeth."[2] The next day he told her to go down to her sister Nannie's and let Nannie's husband pull the rest of her loose teeth to get ready for new ones. On her return she looked in the mirror and had another big cry; her stepmother added to Talula's discomfort by raging and scolding repeatedly. "Your father didn't send you down there to have all your teeth pulled!"[3] Burke had pulled not only the loose teeth but all that were decayed, as John Gilbert had meant that he should. Seeing Talula's distress, her father began planning with her the trip by train from Jonesboro to Atlanta. The healing comfort she felt in her father's assurances and special attention strengthened the bond of love between them and increased Talula's feeling that all would be well.

CHAPTER 6

Amazing Grace

The little plate made in Atlanta must have pleased Talula and restored her good looks, for soon she was receiving formal notes from suitors who "with profound esteem" requested the privilege of corresponding or "the honor of accompanying her to meeting next Sunday."

The fifteen notes and letters and one valentine she saved were from eight different men representing a wide range of backgrounds and circumstances. Her would-be beaux included brash newcomers to the area, "old bachelors" or widowers, and the more eligible sons of families who had first settled the new counties south of Atlanta.

Much can be learned about Talula's inner life, her independent spirit, and strong sense of self-determination from those saved letters and from reflections in her memoir on a dozen other beaux. One of her first requests to correspond came from an "old widower" when she was barely seventeen years old, and it made her "mad." Her first proposal was from young Tom Hill, a beau she continued to see long after she had turned him down. She cried and tore up the letter from an "old bachelor" in his late twenties when he asked her to correspond. She was insulted and denied the presumptuous request of one persistent suitor who in his second note (she had ignored the first) apologized for "the very bold act on my part in writing this letter, but I have fell in love with you." But he tried again with the unforgiveable, "as you denied me the pleasure of corresponding, will you allow me to visit you? . . . Until this request is denied me, I won't give up . . . if you favor me as a Suitor, I will see your father and get his consent." One rejected suitor was later "bitten by a mad dog and died a horrible death." Another married Professor Looney's daughter; "he had his life plastered in him with sticking plaster" and soon died of consumption. Still another decided to pursue first one and then another of the younger Gilbert sisters while waiting for Talula to change her mind. At least once she enlisted the aid of Grandmother Tabitha: "Lou can't go to church with you—she has to stay with me today." She quickly terminated the visits of one suitor when her younger brothers, while the grown folks were at dinner, found a flask of whiskey in his topcoat pocket. "I would never marry a drunkard," she recorded.

As Talula's nineteenth birthday approached, her brother's wife, Etta, and her married sister, Nannie, began urging her to marry one or the other of the most eligible young men. They saw how hard she worked for the family, how her rheumatism grew worse until she would cry with the pain, how often she was kept home even on Sundays to cook dinner while her younger sisters went to church and were escorted home by their beaux. They knew Talula had turned away more than one young man from a "good family" and one well-established in business who could have given her the fine life of a lady in Jonesboro.

Her sister Minta and half-sister Bettie were probably the first to learn why Talula seemed so irrationally determined to remain a slave and, if necessary, an old maid.

"Well," Talula wrote in her Memoir more than three score years later, "I had lots of beaux but didn't like them until once a young fellow with black hair and black eyes came to see me, shyly. I had liked him since childhood and one Sunday, while riding with Tom Hill just after he had asked me to marry him, we met the blackheaded boy riding a pony. Right then and there I decided I'd never marry anyone as long as he was single, tho I didn't know he'd ever come to see me, or ever want me to marry him."[1]

The shy young man was Thomas Jefferson Bottoms, son of Elisa McElroy Bottoms who had been widowed soon after the war and left with insurmountable debts that still threatened the loss of her farm despite the help of her now-grown sons. Tom was the sixteenth child of his father, James Madison Bottoms, who had come to Pike County in the 1820s with his first wife. James had married Elizabeth Lockhart, the daughter of a well-to-do family in North Carolina, when she was barely thirteen years old. Like so many pioneer women of her time, at age seventeen Elizabeth took her two young children and Hannah, a young black woman her wealthy grandfather had given her when both girls were still children, and went with her husband into a wild, unknown land. She bore him six more children

---

Tommie never got to go to school much more until he was about grown. He had to work, as it was not long after the civil war, and times were so hard with the southern people, as all their paper money went dead at the close of the civil war and not many people had silver and gold. They had to spin and weave cloth for all clothes, and then make them by hand when they got them made, they were good, and clothes would last a long time. I can remember the women would cut out garments to make, and would go visiting sometimes in the afternoon, and take their work to sew on. And the little children would go too, to play with other children of the family that were being visited. Those days were good old days. And it seemed that neighbors were so good, and loved each other.

—Talula Bottoms, Memoir

before she died in 1839 at age thirty-one. The young family had lived in the covered wagon until a rough cabin could be built and depended on hunting and fishing to provide food until enough land was cleared for crops and a garden. Elizabeth spun and wove, sewed by hand, and cooked on an open fireplace made of "sticks and dirt." She gave birth to two more children before they could call the 202 acres of land their own, for James had bound himself in an agreement common at that time:

> Georgia, Pike County, Know all men by these presents that James Bottoms am held and firmly bound to James Bell in the final sum of two-hundred dollars for the payment of which I bind myself my heirs etc. this 25th day of August, 1826 . . .
>
> The condition of this obligation is such that if the said James Bottoms shall keep . . . during said term ending the first of March 1829 . . . free from encroachments or intrusions . . until said lease is out, it was given for clearing of land on lot 121st Monroe now Pike County this 25th day of August 1826. Signed James Bottoms (given for Possession).

Saved receipts and legal papers dating from 1821 until James Bottoms's death in November 1866, indicate that he did become a successful cotton planter and that he and his sons operated a sawmill and cotton gin that were widely patronized. But his habits of "binding himself" for credit to buy more land, to run his farms and businesses, and to provide for his large family kept him always in arrears. The records indicate also he was not a Methodist or a Baptist but an independent thinker, a Universalist who had taught himself to read so he could search out his own truth. He was also a man of great generosity to friends and family, freely loaning them money and fiercely determined to leave each of his heirs something to show for his lifelong labors.

Within a few months following Elizabeth's death in 1839 after the birth of her eighth child, James Bottoms had married nineteen-year-old Elisa McElroy of Fayette County. He bought bottom land between Morning Creek and Flint River, soon moved there with his new wife and his seven children, just a few months old to fifteen years, and built the two-room log cabin they would live in the rest of their lives. James and his fifteen-year-old son, John, cut trees and hewed logs for the two main rooms and added a lean-to on one side where the older girls would sleep. They built a big fireplace of "sticks and mud" across one whole end of the kitchen room "that would burn logs six or eight feet long" and lined it inside with stones turned up as they cleared the land. Elisa was proud of that fireplace; it would serve her well for cooking meals for thirty-five years or longer—until the first cast-iron stoves were sold in Fayette County after the War.

James Bottoms continued to travel to Griffin in Pike County in the fall to trade his cotton and pork, also the lard Elisa made in a black pot in the back yard. He traded them for cloth and dye, coffee and sugar, for wine, and for gallon jugs of whiskey, an essential ingredient in folk remedies for everything from babies' colic to old folks' rheumatism. Those trips enabled him to aid his son John who had returned to Pike County, married young and taken over his father's sawmill there. John died in 1859 at 34, leaving a wife, five young children, and heavy debts that James Bottoms helped the young mother repay.

At her husband's death in 1866, Elisa was left with just one grown son, George Washington, the only one of James Bottoms's four grown sons to survive the War, and three young sons, ages six to fifteen. Elisa managed somehow until the late 1870s, when hard times and the burden of debt threatened loss of her 350-acre farm. By then her youngest son, Tom, was almost twenty, still living with her in the old log cabin that had been expanded and covered over with wooden planks, and working the farm. He would not have even "a horse, bridle and saddle" of his own until he reached his twenty-first birthday. He had never been able to attend school regularly and by age fifteen had essentially stopped going so he could work the farm and support his mother.

A young man with so little education, no property, and without even a horse and buggy of his own would not be considered a proper match for one of the Gilbert girls. Both Analiza and Etta—Talula's sister-in-law—almost violently disapproved of him; Nannie had been so outspoken she had driven Talula to tears. But Talula persisted in encouraging the shy young man who never wrote her one of those polite formal notes, and Tom managed on occasion to be the first at her side when preaching was over at the Baptist church. She would, of course, accept his quiet offer to carry her home in his mother's buggy, no matter what other man might be waiting for her outside the church door with his own fine horse and buggy. Then Tom would accept her invitation to stay for dinner with her family, despite Analiza's disapproval.

Perhaps it was because these two were so much alike in spirit that their courtship moved at a snail's pace and, even after they became engaged, was more than once almost terminated. In each ran an undercurrent of resistance to false pride and social pretensions, a strong sense of self-determination, and an integrity rooted in their sincere acceptance of the simple Baptist faith so fervently expounded by preachers they loved and trusted.

It was Analiza who had begun taking her stepchildren as well as her own to the Baptist meeting on first Sunday in Fayetteville, the church founded by the Murphys, Talula's own mother's people. Talula went willingly as well with her father to Methodist meeting on other Sundays. She sat through long, dramatic, and often fiery sermons, learned about sin and salvation, was baptized so often in those dread warnings she began to feel the need for repentance.

It was at "protracted meeting" time in August of her eighteenth year at one of those churches that, as Talula later recalled, "I had begun to think I was a great sinner, and I resolved to get forgiveness for my sins . . . tho decided not to join the church right then but wait and see if I kept feeling as I did. . . ." She tried "while picking beans one day" to talk with her stepmother about her feelings. Talula didn't "remember what she said but not much of anything."[2] It was several months later at an evening service at the newly constituted Corinth Church in Gilbert Schoolhouse (and no doubt young Tom Bottoms was there; for he, his mother, and his brothers were charter members), that Talula was deeply moved by a duet sung by two young sisters, her cousins: "Oh, who will come and go with me, I am bound for the promised land."

Still, Talula waited "until I felt I could hold out to live right." Late in the Fall of 1880 she made the commitment within her own heart and then publicly confessed her faith in the schoolhouse at the new Missionary Baptist Church of Corinth.[3]

It was not until the following May "because the preacher was kindly sickly" that she was immersed in the waters of Morning Creek which ran between the Gilbert and Bottoms farms. Tom Bottoms's brother Bob led the singing for the little band of people gathered on the bank of that muddy stream for the baptizing, and the song that most affected her, Talula remembered, was "Amazing Grace, how sweet the sound, that saved a wretch like me!" When she went home, she tore off the flap of an old envelope and marked the page of that song in the little leather-bound book of one thousand hymns she had "bought at Corinth Church on Sept. 19, 1880, when it was constituted."[4] It was a book whose pages would be worn and tear-stained until the words of many of those old hymns had become as much a part of her as her own heartbeat.

CHAPTER 7

Hesitation

Talula waited and wondered until she was a bit angry with Tom because he did not mention marriage to her. She knew no other woman interested him, and they had an unspoken agreement that he would carry her home from the Baptist meeting twice a month and to all day singing on Fifth Sunday. Beyond that, she had no assurance he would ever ask her to be his wife.

With three daughters of marriageable age in John Gilbert's household, young men were frequent callers, and Tom did not seem to mind that Talula allowed one or the other of them to escort her when it was not his Sunday. Yet she knew she would never marry anyone of her present acquaintance except Tom Bottoms. As a matter of practical fact, too, she knew she didn't want the life of an old maid, "to be left dancing in the dog-trot" when her younger sisters were married. Trapped in that household with so much work to do for the family, she was frightened to think she would never have time to fill her trunk with her own quilts and other things made by her own hands that she would need if ever Tom did ask her to marry him. Even if she could finish the nice quilts she had started, when would she ever be allowed time to quilt them? Analiza, often with help of neighbor women, did all the practical quilting for the family, while Talula's rheumatism grew worse from the heavy housework that must be done. No matter how hard she tried to please her stepmother, Analiza's inevitable explosions of temper spoiled all Talula's efforts and often drove her to tears.

As laying-by time approached in July 1881, Talula did a bold thing. She wrote to her cousin John Rogers who lived up toward Chattanooga at Rogers Station. She invited him to bring a friend, a Mr. Smith he had told her about, to spend a week with her family and attend protracted meeting at Corinth Church, for she wanted to meet him. Did she have in mind showing Tom she had her limits in waiting for a proposal, or was it simply a healthy reaching out from her tight world to a wider one?

"Cousin Lula," John replied in his August first letter, "I'm sorry that I can't come and bring Mr. Smith . . . we never stop work when crops are finished; if anything we work harder—we are fixing to build a milltrace. . . . It would be better for you to come up to see us next month—and then you could meet him. Our meeting protracts the 3rd Saturday in August. Tell [your brother] Matthew to come and bring you and spend a few weeks. I have no doubt it would be an advantage to yours and Matthew's health—I can insure you a good time—being so many young ladies and men here . . . and they are so lively. . . ."

Whether Talula ever met Mr. Smith is not known, but when Tom finally proposed abruptly and with no romantic pretensions in the fall of 1881, it so surprised Talula she could find no words with which to respond. Although she was profoundly moved, all she could say was, "Well, I'll study about it." Tom was considerably taken aback after all his months of anguished restraint, having waited until as close to his twenty-first birthday in December as he thought would give her time to make preparations to be married. It was then he would come into possession of the "horse, bridle and saddle" his father's will had given him, and he would have paid for the fifty acres of land he had bought from one of his older brothers by working in his sawmill business. He had never explained his plans to her, but there were reasons for Talula's "studying" about marriage before she plunged in with Tom or anyone else. In her Memoir so many years later she reflects:

> It was hard for me to decide what to do . . . as I had been told by my stepmother that if I married, I would take consumption and die like my mother and my aunt . . . I was a weakly little girl . . . and I got stronger, and have lived with the one I liked best to be 81 years old, and hope I can live with him longer.[1]

The courtship rocked on precariously for nearly a year until Tom's seeming indifference alarmed Talula. After much painful reflection, she talked to her father and discovered he had more respect for Tom Bottoms than "all the rest that could stand between here and Morning Creek." She found it very awkward trying finally to let Tom know she was ready to say yes, and was

Right then and there I decided that I'd never marry anyone as long as he was single, tho I didn't know that he'd ever come to see me, or ever want me to marry him, but I did not want anyone, but him. So finally he came to see me, but he seemed kindly shy.
—Talula Bottoms, Memoir

Thomas Jefferson Bottoms (right) at age 17, with his nephew age 33, who became like a father to Tom after his own father, James Bottoms, died in 1866. The photograph was made from a tintype taken in 1878 in Jonesboro, Georgia, when brotherly love between men could be expressed without suspicion, unlike today. Tom was the "shy black-headed boy" Talula had "liked since childhood." They were "tied up in the marriage vow" in a simple home ceremony on February 23, 1883, after a rocky courtship of more than two years. Then they drove in Tom's own buggy to his mother's log cabin home where they would live for fifteen years until they moved to Sand Mountain, Alabama.

embarrassed and dismayed when he then put *her* off because "times is so hard now, maybe we better wait awhile." When Talula again began accepting the attentions of Tom Hill and Bob Crittenden, the "old bachelor" who had gone out with all three of her sisters and recently returned from Dubois, Georgia, Tom Bottoms decided—hard times or not—he must take matters into his own strong hands. Quite suddenly he came up with a ring. He approached her in such a stern and confident manner after church one Sunday in May 1882, that Talula walked right out the door with him past Bobbie Crittenden who had already asked to take her home that day.

Despite her almost casual dismissal of her long friendship with Bob Crittenden in her memoir, Talula saved two letters from him. In one dated May 27, 1882, after having been deeply hurt, he tells her so, begs forgiveness for writing without her permission, and expresses "hope that your future pathway will be amid the sweetest flowers of happiness, and not yours only, but your good little sister's, Miss Mintie's. The other, a five-page letter dated August 6, is proof positive this long-time suitor had not yet given up hope. He had been back to Fayette County to attend a wedding and while there "heard that you had your *sure enough ring* but disputed it because I never saw you wear it . . .," heard also about some "little difference with that fellow . . . and why not tell him it would be best for you and him to be friends only . . . To be plane with you Miss Lula, [marriage] is a great and important [decision], it is for life & we should try to make a wise choice . . . for if there is a mistake we have the trouble to beair . . ." He pleads a strong case for himself and closes with "I will ever keep very sacred what you write to me . . . I am still your true Friend Bobbie C."

Whatever the "little difference" may have been, when Tom's visits stopped abruptly sometime in the fall of that year, and Talula looked in vain for several weeks to find him across the aisle on the men's side in church, a terrible fear overcame her. What had she done? What could she do? No proper lady could without shame and disgrace make the first move to clear up any misunderstanding in such a situation. Humiliation kept her from approaching even her younger sisters Bettie and Minta until they began to notice how often she came in from milking or from the garden with her eyes red from crying, and how she quickly tried to hide her tears if they asked her about Tom.

When Talula could stand it no longer, she enlisted the aid of her sister Bettie, pledging her to absolute secrecy. Together they violated that sacred code of proper conduct for a woman; Talula wrote Tom a letter apologizing for whatever offense she may have committed and assuring him he was welcome if he wanted to call on her again. She sent the letter to be secretly posted by Bettie, whose turn it was to go to Jonesboro with her father next day.

This time Tom insisted there be no more delays. Hasty preparations were made for a wedding at the Gilbert home in less than two weeks, much sooner than Talula thought she could be ready.

Tom's visits had stopped because he had split his foot open with an axe and was ashamed to be seen hobbling about, even to church, on his homemade crutches. He didn't write Talula a note or send her word because he had believed she needed to "study about" getting married. He didn't want any doubts afterward. He must have laughed heartily, even proudly, when he received her note. It showed she was not a slave to society's pretensions any more than he. But Tom kept her secret and the letter; it was saved by Talula until they had a houseful of children. By the time her daughter Mollie Ruth learned from her older sister about her mother's bold gesture, Talula could laugh about it. In 1940 Talula recalls:

> I kept the letter for a long time, 'till the children found it in my trunk and then I burned it up. I wouldn't a had them read it for anything in the world. That is why sister knew about it and told you. Before that, I had never said anything to a soul about writing that letter, but I guess it's a good thing I wrote it.[2]

CHAPTER 8

Awakening

Talula Gilbert and Tom Bottoms were married on February 21, 1883, six days after her twenty-first birthday. Tom would not be twenty-three until December. They were "tied up in the marriage vow" in the front room of the Gilbert home by "the distinguished Dr. Issac G. Woolsey, Baptist Minister, Medical doctor, farmer and landowner,"[1] and one of the most influential men in Fayette County. He and Mrs. Woolsey stayed for the wedding supper, which was "nothing to compare with the one . . . for Nannie" eight years earlier. Neither was there a big infare the next day, for the Bottoms were simple country folk and times were hard. How hard Talula would soon find out.

Talula did not get to take one of her own mother's nice quilts with her, though the Gilbert beds were no doubt covered with them for her wedding. As was the custom, Talula and Tom slept their first night together in the big front room at her father's house where they were married and drove next day after the wedding breakfast to his mother's house with Tom's own horse hitched to the buggy.

Talula's trunk was not filled with the many quilts she had only dreamed of making; she took with her in a little trunk her father gave her only one finished quilt, completed "at nights and little odd times," and one unquilted top. But in her head danced the designs of a dozen pretty quilts she longed to make, and would, as soon as she was settled into her new life with this man she loved.

Within two weeks after her marriage, Talula discovered the shocking truth about why Tom had been reluctant to marry for so long. His mother was in imminent danger of losing all her "Goods and Chattels, Lands and Tenements" because of notes she had signed with two older sons for operation of the farm and to cover losses sustained in their failed sawmill business. At

Tommie said he was going to Alabama with his people if he didn't stay at the home place. So I went over to my father's house, and I told him what Tommie had said, and he didn't want us to go to Alabama. So he got busy and bought the old Bottoms home and gave it to us, to keep us there in Georgia. We were glad of the old home. It was a pretty place and a good place to live. We lived happily there, only when Tommie would have fever, for he got to having malaria most every year and sometimes twice a year.

—Talula Bottoms, Memoir

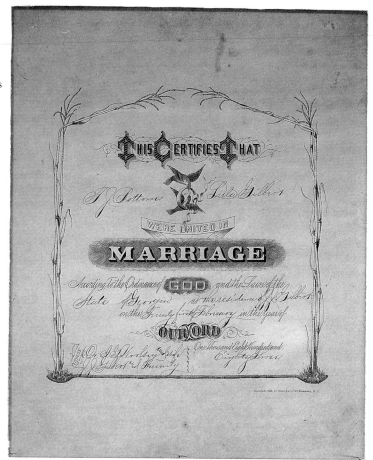

Marriage certificate of Thomas Bottoms and Talula Gilbert, February 21, 1883.

least a dozen summons to appear in court were issued to E. M. Bottoms and her sons in 1883, some of them by Mr. Frank Blalock, justice of the peace, who had bought up some of the notes. He and others were about to foreclose for the sum of $553.07 owed by them. Tom felt it his "boundened duty" to sacrifice his own "chattel" too—now that he was of legal age— if it would save anything for his mother. She and Tom were able to scrape up a few dollars here and there and make small payments to bide some time, but within a year the disaster was inevitable. It seemed that all James Bottoms had worked forty years for, and Elisa and her sons had tried fifteen more years to save, would be lost; there was nothing to do but let the place go. Tom was sure he could go somewhere and make a fresh start. He talked of moving to Sand Mountain, Alabama, where "people could inter [*sic*] a place by paying $18 for an intery of 160 acres with sometimes a small house and a few acres cleared." Several of James Bottoms's descendants had already migrated to that sandstone plateau in northern Alabama where the Appalachian range trails off toward Mississippi. Georgia farmers for several years had received glowing reports of the fine sandy soil and healthy air of the new county of Cullman on Brindley Mountain, the westernmost extension of that plateau called Sand Mountain. It was reported to be the healthiest place in the United States; even Tom's brother James Madison Bottoms talked of moving there with his family from the log cabin they had occupied on Elisa's place since his remarried sister, Sarah, and her two sons, George Washington and James Franklin Walker, had moved to Alabama.

Talula hoped it was all just talk, that Tom wouldn't go, but how could she help feeling anger and resentment toward him for not having warned her about his difficulties? She had learned the grim facts from her sister-in-law (James Madison's wife) soon after her marriage to the "only one she had ever liked." But even then she never dreamed there would be cause to move so far away and leave all she knew of love and security. She was utterly heartsick at the thought of leaving brothers and sisters, her good father, and her aging, almost blind, Grandmother Tabitha. And she couldn't conceive of being so far removed from the church that had nurtured and sustained her faith, where so many tears of repentance and joy had been shed.

Now she realized fully why her family had disapproved of Tom. They had pointed out to her he had "no business sense," but then she had resolved to rule him! Now she wondered too whether, if they were to move away, she would become old and bitter like so many farm women who had to work in the field, chopping or picking cotton, or haying, or whatever the farm seasons required. She had known the Bottoms women worked in the fields alongside their husbands and sons, but she did not know that her father had spoken to Tom about that when he had asked John Gilbert's permission to marry his daughter. He had warned Tom that she wasn't a strong woman and might never be able to have children. He had asked Tom not to let his daughter work in the fields, and Tom had promised.

As Talula wrestled with these new trials and the feelings they prompted, did she look again at the old tablet on which she had scrawled in pencil years before that had helped her endure the hardships she had already surmounted? The brittle, yellowed paper was found in a box of old letters Talula gave to her daughter Mollie Ruth in the 1940's:

> Health, I will keep my body clean and healthful. Will keep all mental poisens out of my thoughts. Will especially resist and exclude fear which weakens and unnerves me. Will adjust to

When I grew up and married, I hadn't had the chance to make myself quilts much, and as I loved to piece and work on my quilt work, I decided to put in every moment of my time that I was not busy at something that was needed more, I'd work on my quilt work when I could get the material to work with.

—Talula Bottoms, Memoir

whatever happens. Will not worry. If a thing can be helped, I will help it; if not, I will make the best of it.

Congenial work: If I cannot find something to do that is pleasant, will try to find pleasure in what I am doing. I will be honest, square, prompt and thoughtful, will try to do somebody a good turn everyday.

Discipline of self-controle I will not allow myself to become angry. Will resist pride. If any person treats me wrong I will not bear him a grudge. Will try to forget it. Will manage to get along without friction or quarrel or strained relations with my family, my friends, neighbors and others. Will cultivate good habits, I will strive to force my will to obey God's laws. [3]

She had needed to live by that code in her father's house. If she thought she had learned thrift well enough there, she was often reminded she had not. Perhaps now she looked again at the little note she had saved from her sister Minta written while they were both still children:

This Thursday Morning

Dear Sister Lula,
I write this little note to inform you that ma wants you to be more saving . . . she thinks you have been wasting . . . we picked the geese yesterday and while I was (out) catching a goose, ma found that the preserves was untied . . . ma said not give them (the younger children) any milk to drink (either) . . .

Your sister MMG[4]

If Talula re-read her sister's note then, it must have reminded her of an incident soon after her marriage and made her aware of how much she had yet to learn of thrift, and of learning to please her new mother. She had pitched in to help with the cooking and knew she had made the finest possible buttermilk biscuits—three times a day—as she had done at home. But Elisa was not pleased, nor was Tom. Finally he told her they could afford biscuits only for breakfast. The other meals must be cornbread. They had not wanted to hurt her feelings, but Tom had had to tell her after his Mother told him that the flour was getting low and there was no more wheat to take to mill, and no money to buy it.

When, with foreclosure imminent in early October 1884, Tom told Talula he would be going to Alabama within a month to help his brother move and that he meant to look for a place of his own, it did not take Talula long to "resist and exclude the fear" that might "weaken and unnerve" her. She knew her fa-

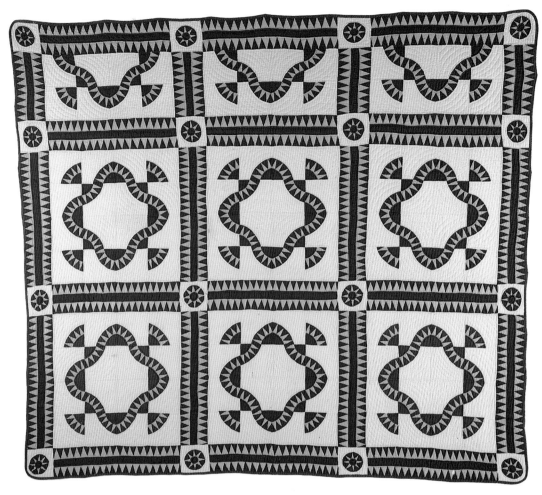

Baby Bunting, above, c. late 1870's–1880's (pattern No. 493 in *Quilt Patterns,* leaflet among Talula's patterns). This is thought to be the one quilt Talula had quilted to take with her when she married Tom Bottoms in 1883. Its nearly 4,000 triangles speak movingly of patience, determination, and developing skill. The entire quilt is made by hand, and the quality of the workmanship marks it as a learning piece. It is filled with hand-carded cotton, and the quilting is evidence no skilled quilter has helped her learn how to avoid knots and backstitches. In many places she has made turns awkwardly or incompletely, even overlooking completion of the quilting of a little sunburst or line of points in the sashing. The half-squares at the top were made to go just to the pillows to save cloth, and still not appear incomplete. *Left:* Detail of *Baby Bunting.*

ther would be as heartsick as herself at having his daughter move away, so the day after the sheriff had handed Tom the dreaded final foreclosure notice, Talula crossed Morning Creek bridge and walked the two miles up the dirt road to her father's house.

John Gilbert promptly paid off all the notes and saved Elisa's farm himself, expecting to give it to his daughter as part of her inheritance when he was gone.

It must have been some small relief to Tom and Elisa Bottoms to know they wouldn't be compelled to move or remain only to pay rent to Mr. Blalock, but when Elisa began taking all her quilts out of her trunk and packing to go to Alabama with her son James and his family, both Tom and Talula were stunned and bewildered. Tom could not conceive of surviving on that lowland farm without this strong mother by his side. And how humiliating for him to realize all he had of his own to offer his wife was "a horse, bridle and saddle" and fifty acres of swampy bottom land down by Morning Creek! Therefore he went on as planned and drove one of the covered wagons to Alabama with his courageous mother by his side. Elisa insisted she was going because Laura, her daughter-in-law, was expecting another child. "I can't let her go off in that condition by herself," she said. Tom suspected, however, there was a deeper, more troubling reason that his mother was too proud to voice. Before she left, she called together all her daughters-in-law and divided among them her trunk full of quilts.

The first letter Tom had ever written to Talula came from Coloma, Alabama, at the end of November and made her heart glad. "As to the country I have not seen any that I like as well as I do Fayette County," he wrote, and signed the letter "Your devoted husband. T. J. Bottoms." Though she knew he loved her, he had never before uttered one word signifying love or devotion, and it was almost worth the fear and loneliness of this first separation to read that letter. She felt sure, too, it meant they would never have to move to Alabama.

Coloma, Ala.   Nov. 25, 1884
Lula Dear wife I take my Seat to write you a few lines to let you know how we have got along we are travling very slow but we have been well all the time we camped in the river swamp the first night we have not lay out since we got to Mr. Famby's, last night we have traveld about about 20 miles a day we don't know when we will get there you need not look for me until you see me I have no news to write as to the country I have not seen any that I lik as well as I do Fayette Co. Shew this to Sam's folks as soon as you can. George is going with us to the mountain as nothing esls to write I will close Your devoted husband

—T. J. Bottoms

CHAPTER 9

Realization

Despite the uncertainties and shocks of that first year as a married woman, Talula must have enjoyed a new sense of freedom and often counted her blessings. With two efficient women sharing the work of gardening, milking, raising chickens, cooking, washing, and ironing, and fewer people to do it for, both Talula and Elisa found more time to work on quilts. As they leaned over the big quilting frame balanced on four chair backs to quilt Talula's *Magnolia Leaf* in little pairs and quadruples of hearts, or worked Elisa's scrap quilt in big arcs, Talula's rheumatism began to subside. Before the year was out she was, for the first time since early childhood, free of the pain and swelling in her ankles and feet.

Talula became the willing student of a skilled quilter and began to make up for lost time when she could "get the material to work with." For the first year no money could be spared for new cloth to make anything, but Elisa improvised with the tiniest scraps and pieces of old clothes to create consistent patterns for pretty blocks. She dyed feed sacks to join them together for everyday quilts anyone would be proud to use. Talula might once have called that scrimping, but Elisa had known nothing except hard times since the War. She became for Talula a master teacher not only of quilting, but of frugality and resourcefulness. Talula learned well those lessons in thrift and improvisation, and the proof lies in her many scrap quilts remaining today. During the eight years she spent in close and intimate proximity with Elisa, Talula's skills as efficient housekeeper and quiltmaker were fully developed.

The years after Talula's father saved his mother's farm were not easy for Tom, but life had never been easy for him. He had suffered intermittently from malaria since childhood, but now his attacks became worse. On the trip to Cullman, Alabama, in November 1884, he had driven a mule team hitched to one of the two covered wagons carrying all his brother James's worldly

Talula's *Magnolia Leaf,* c. 1880s, is similar to *Oak Leaf and Reel,* pictured in *American Quilts and Coverlets,* by Carleton L. Safford and Robert Bishop. This may have been the quilt top that Talula had made but did not have time to quilt before her marriage. The blocks were probably sewed together by a hand-turned machine and the binding attached the same way, then turned over and whipped down on the back. The workmanship is not so fine as that seen in her later quilts, but much better than in the *Baby Bunting.* The bridal motif of hearts in the quilting suggests she quilted it soon after her marriage with the help of her mother-in-law Elisa, a fine quilter in her own right. The borders on just two sides of the quilt are evidence it was made for a special front room bed pushed into a corner and used only on rare occasions. This quilt and the *Baby Bunting* have stayed together through the years and have now been passed on to one of Talula's great-granddaughters.

goods, and with hope in his heart, for no case of malaria had ever been reported there. When he returned, the possibility of a move was not ruled out; however, Tom knew he wouldn't make the move just then. He could not tear Talula away from her family, and he felt obliged to his father-in-law, who thought he had done Tom a favor in saving Elisa's farm.

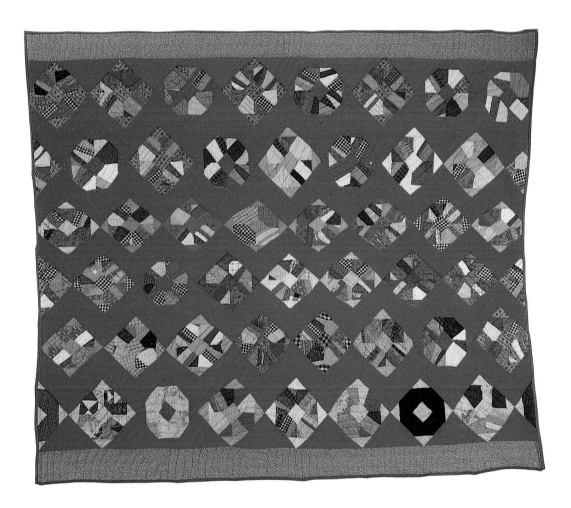

String Quilt Variation (c. 1875–1890) This depression-type quilt utilizing scraps from old clothes was made for everyday and used often (note shell quilting). The blocks were pieced with great ingenuity to maintain the pattern that looks like a double bow tie. Put together with Turkey red strips in an overall zig-zag pattern, it was probably made by Elisa McElroy Bottoms. A similar pattern called *Wishing Ring*, not a string quilt, appeared in the *Kansas City Star*, mid-twentieth century. (Information courtesy Barbara Brackman of Lawrence, Kansas.) Talula's letter to daughter Mollie Ruth (September, 1940) suggests this may have been one of the "poorest bunch" of quilts her beloved mother-in-law made. The fact that such a "common" quilt was preserved, and in such fine condition, marks it as a treasured heirloom.

Tom turned his strong energies to making a go of the farm, and to Corinth Church, which meant so much to him, his mother, and Talula. After the sawmill failed in 1882, the hands that already had been hired were put to sawing lumber for a new church for the little congregation that was still meeting in the old Gilbert Schoolhouse made of logs. It was Tom's brother Bobbie's desire to donate the lumber to that church where he had been the first pastor and to have the men of the church build it. Ironically, that generous gesture created even greater burdens of debt—the ultimate cause of Elisa's bankruptcy—but the family took heart from seeing that church rise out of the ashes of their defeat. Tom became a deacon, and the church stands there today, a monument to the determination of the Bottoms family, their faith and lifted spirits.

The first time Talula and Tom were left alone together in their own home was a wholly new experience for her. With Mother Elisa gone to Alabama to be with James Madison's wife, who was expecting a child in February, Talula could now manage her own household, and she began to save up eggs and butter to buy new material for quilts. She did it unobtrusively, for she feared Tom would think it an extravagance. Those commodities, hard earned by her own work, were normally used to barter for essentials. She remembered the winter when, at sixteen, responsible for the cooking and baking, she had saved enough eggs (by hiding them from her stepmother) to buy red opera flannel and nice trimming for a pretty sack for herself. Then how proud she had been to wear it when she went visiting overnight, or for an occasional week with cousins or friends! Her stepmother's sister, "Aunt Mollie" Tarpley, had made it for her—full and flowing, with lace ruffles at the neck and sleeves. Now, although she was still wearing that well-worn dressing gown and had only one dress—the black one in which she had been married—to wear to church and singings with Tom, she wanted new material for quilts more than anything, and oh, how she did enjoy being mistress of her own home![1]

One Sunday when they had planned a visit with her family, Talula learned there were limits to her being mistress of that household. They began with her strong-willed husband. Tom had stopped shaving before Christmas soon after returning from Atlanta where he'd gone to sell his cotton. He had bought a fine new razor guaranteed not to pull and hurt his face when he shaved. He never would tell her how much he paid for it, but

Talula knew it was enough to buy lots of cloth. When she heard him explode in anger while he was shaving himself to get ready for meeting one Sunday morning, she was at a loss to know how to manage such an outburst. He had fussed and fumed and strapped the new razor until it seemed the old razor strap would be worn out. After that he refused to use it and, regardless of her protests, began to let his whiskers grow.

When Talula was an old woman she could look back and laugh as she recorded in her Memoir what happened a few weeks later:

> One Sunday I wanted to go to my father's house and I beged him to shave and lets go, and he wouldn't do it, and I beged and beged but it did no good. So I had to give it up, and he has never shaved since, tho his (grown) boys (caught him sleeping in his chair and) shaved him once to see how he looked . . . so I soon learned who was boss and (after that) I didn't want to rule him.[2]

Not long after that incident, Tom walked over to his brother George's house and gave him the razor. (George Washington's granddaughter Sarah Barber laughed as she gently pulled out the blade of that fine old-fashioned razor in 1985 and told the story.[3]) George Washington soon began to let his whiskers grow, too, and so did James Madison Bottoms over in Alabama. But contrary to Talula's recollection, Thomas Jefferson's long beard was cut three times, and his children saved them all. Even today, one or another of Tom's grandchildren has refused to allow those long beards, one auburn, one grey, and one white mounted on a strong board, to be destroyed.

Some time after Tom had established himself as head of his house, even though it legally belonged to his wife's father, Talula joyfully realized she was pregnant. It seemed to her the most wonderful thing that had ever happened. She knew, though he never mentioned it, how proud Tom was, how he had longed for some boys of his own; even one son would be such a help to him on the farm. She settled down to sewing baby clothes while she finished piecing the quilts she had in process and was filled with radiant happiness as she awaited the great mystery.

We never had to buy food only flour, sugar and coffe, as we grew it all at home. Also our hogs for meat and lard. We had a lot of good sausage too. We had no canned goods to eat so most of our food was biscuit, meat and gravy also syrup and butter and milk. The gravy would be thickened gravy sometimes. Tho for dinner we had some kind of boiled victuals. In winter it was mostly dry peas with meat boiled with them or turnip greens or collards, as we could have all kinds of greens thru the winters, as there were no bugs of any kind to bother them in those good days.

—Talula Bottoms, Memoir

Unnamed scrap quilt, *above,*
c. 1875–1890, called *Vice-President's
Quilt* in *Quilt Patterns,* Ladies Art
Co., 1928 catalogue of over 500
quilt patterns found among Talula's
things. This is another depression-
type quilt, utilizing some of the
same fabrics as Elisa Bottoms's String
quilt on page 73 though each "bow"
in this quilt is pieced of one fabric
instead of many. The squares are put
together with pieced feed sacks,
home-dyed pink and green, perhaps
once red and green. The hand
carded cotton batting is very thick,
and the backing is store bought,
suggesting the quilt top was made
during very hard times and quilted
later, perhaps by Talula after Elisa's
death. *Right:* Detail of scrap quilt.

CHAPTER 10

To Bend in Meek Submission

The old log house began to creak and groan as the earth trembled under it. The windows rattled and the black iron stove shrieked and danced on its feet. As Talula awoke from a tormented sleep in the middle of the nightmare and reached for the lamp, she knew something was terribly wrong. The flame weaved and smoked, and when she got off the bed the floor rocked under her feet. Then she remembered as she stumbled into the next room that her first baby son lay gravely ill; she had been so exhausted, the others watching at the bedside had persuaded her to lie down on the kitchen cot and try to get some sleep.

Next day they learned the worst of the earthquake was at Charleston, South Carolina, but all the way to Fayette County the rumbling and shaking terrified people and reminded them of the power of God. They said folks in Charleston had not been living as they ought or such a thing would not have come upon them.

Nine-month-old Johnny died just before dawn on that September first, 1886, and Talula and Tom were plunged into sorrow such as they had never known possible. They, too, searched their souls for what they had done wrong. Tom wept with great heaving sobs, but Talula's grief was frozen in a heavy lump that seemed caught in the bottom of her heart.

She could not cry even as she heard Tom sawing boards and pounding in the nails to make the little wooden coffin, nor as the stricken family gathered after the sad funeral at the edge of the farm to lower the little box into its small grave in the family cemetery. It was not until she was writing the final words of the obituary to send to the *Christian Index,* the first she had ever

Talula felt her own limitations in composing an obituary for her infant son and thought her handwriting so poor, she showed the first twenty-one lines she had written to her sister Minta and asked her to copy it over and write something more suitable to be sent to the paper. Minta, however, was ill, and could not "compose herself" to do more than copy off the few lines Talula had written. She sent instead the poem, "We Saw not the White Robed Angel." Talula then finished the piece she had begun trying with all her might to write as legibly as her sister:

> Little Johnny—died of cholera inphantom Sept. 1st 1886 in Fayette County Ga. John James infant son and only child of T. J. and Lula Bottoms. Was born January 1st, 1886, 8 months.
>
> He was just a little tender bud loaned to us for a short while here on earth but we feel that we have a stronger tie with Jesus now. Our little darling, a gift from God, has awakened in Paradise where sickness, suffering and parting shall never enter. Our home is made very lonely and sad. We cannot see those bright eyes nor hear that sweet voice again on earth. He had a serious and sensible Countenance and was a good babe—yes, too good to stay here with us; our Heavenly Father saw fit to take him home. Oh! how sad that we have to part with our loved ones so soon, yet what a sweet consolation to know that we are all on our way. We know not when we, too, may end our journey, therefore let us strive to be ready to meet our Master when he shall come. While we can't help but mourn for little Johnny, yet why should we grieve when we know that he is so much better off than any of us now in that peaceful home with his little hands outstretched beckoning to us, and calling us Homeward. While we can't and would not call him back to us, we can strive ever to be ready to meet him on that beautiful shore, where we never shall weep or part anymore.

tried to compose, that she began to cry and feel a melting of the heavy pain inside her heart.

Just a few weeks earlier, she had thought her world was as full of happiness as it ever could be. Johnny had come to bless their home on January first that year, and throughout the spring and early summer all nature seemed to sing with her for the very joy of living. She had learned that Elisa's silence as she moved briskly about her work did not mean disapproval; so Talula was no longer shy about singing, or humming familiar hymns as she cared for the baby and cooked or gardened or sewed.

Already she had made "five or six nice pretty quilt tops" and had graduated from needing Elisa's help to borrowing quilts she admired from anyone she could, and drafting her own patterns to make them. She began by borrowing a quilt from her stepmother's sister, Mary Tarpley, one much admired in the area, the *Rocky Mountain*. Like her own earlier quilt, the *Baby Bunting*, it required piecing thousands of tiny triangles and sewing them into curved patches difficult indeed for a beginning quilter. Then she "got the patterns of all [her] own mother's

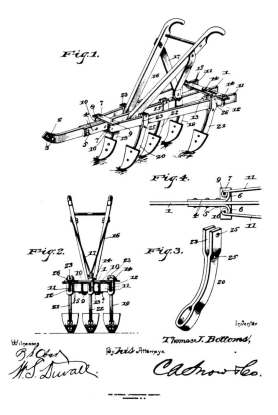

(No Model.)

T. J. BOTTOMS.
COMBINATION CULTIVATOR.

No. 508,912. Patented Nov. 21, 1893.

Guano Distributor, *above*. Tom Bottoms was an inventive thinker and tireless worker, but his inventions for all his hard work never brought him more than a few dollars, and that from other "poor dirt farmers" like himself. Bound to the simple, unsophisticated folkways of his time and place, he was limited by his innocence; yet he knew his ideas were good. It was son Roger who punctured his father's illusions of ever making a great deal of money by patenting and marketing his inventions. Tom then abandoned that dream and turned his energies to perfecting his long-grained cotton and marketing the seed. *Left*: Detail of patent drawings for Combination Cultivator.

nice quilts," and even drafted the pattern of the difficult, wholly pieced *Orange Bud* that good quilters of the area prided themselves in being able to sew into perfect squares.

She had a little leather-covered trunk that had been her father's, and it was there she would fold away the quilt tops as she completed them to save until she had time to put up the big frame and quilt them. She pieced or appliquéd the blocks and sewed most of them together by hand, although Elisa had a sewing machine that "sat on a little table, with a crank on the right side to turn it." Talula had used that to hem sheets and diapers and to make gowns for the baby, but she wouldn't have dreamed of sewing his dresses except by hand, trimming them with dainty white embroidery and her own crocheted edging.

The first glass fruit cans that came about I was grown, and Mr. McElroy was the first to get them in our neighborhood. I could not imagine how he canned his fruit, tho before very many years after we were married we got ½ dozen quart glass jars to can in. So I canned peaches in them as I was already married and had little children about four or five of them, So one night the preacher was with us and I opened a quart jar of the fruit for supper, and as it was a rare thing I told the little children to not ask for it but once and after awhile one of the little boys ask for a second helping of the fruit and another little boy hallowed out "Mama he has had some once and ask for more." I said nothing, tho, for I was ashamed of the children.

—Talula Bottoms, Memoir

Now Talula set about the task of folding away Johnny's clothes for the next baby, for already she was "in the family way" again. It was perhaps the anticipation of another little one that kept Tom and her from being overwhelmed with grief. They went to church together and lifted their repentant hearts to God; without doubt, Talula turned increasingly to her quilt piecing for comfort and tried through the work of her hands to learn to "bend in meek submission" to her Heavenly Father's will. Before long she would appliqué a *Feather* like her favorite of Elisa's.

Tom was caught in an economic bind with other small farmers all over the South. They had no control over the low prices paid for hard-earned commodities, and the high prices required to transport or store them. Even cloth, made from the very cotton so laboriously produced, was high.

His mother, who had kept the old loom, began weaving again to save money. He wished his mother and his wife could go to Jonesboro or Atlanta and buy nice material for clothes and quilting, but their weaving did bring back fond memories of boyhood. Tom was continually frustrated, too, trying to make even a poor living on the farm that was no longer even his mother's. He had already considered and dismissed several other pursuits; now he began to feel he should study to become a preacher.

In 1884 he had helped organize the Morning Creek Farmer's Alliance. He had pooled his strength and resources with other farmers to build a big warehouse in Fayetteville to store cotton until prices were right, and after a tornado destroyed it, he had helped rebuild it with his own hands. He had run for county commissioner on the Populist ticket, had thought of a political career and would be appointed delegate to the state convention in 1892. Before that he had thought he wanted to be a doctor, but his severely practical mother soon got that notion out of his head. At age twenty, with not even a grade-school education and a living to earn, she reminded him, and "no money to be had anywhere in Georgia since the war," his future lay in his own two hands and what he could do with them. He knew how to make things grow, and he could build almost anything needed at home or on the farm, with axe, saw, hammer, and nails, so he set about inventing improvements on the crude farm implements they had.

Yet he remembered still with some anguish that he meant to have a thriving farm of his own someday and, if it pleased his

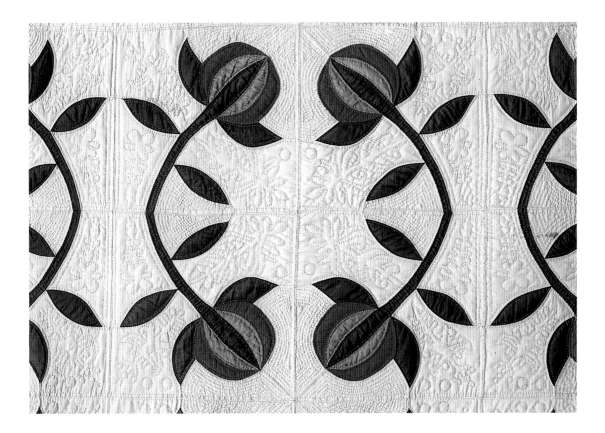

"The Orange bud quilt [of my Mother's] that my stepmother said was hers went to sister Bettie Stell, and I borrowed it, got the patterns [drafted them from the finished quilt] and made one like it and I quilted it nice . . . ," Talula wrote in her Memoir. She gave the *Orange Bud* to her oldest son, Ary, and it was subsequently lost or worn out. Her mother's (or Analiza's) quilt has not been found. Interestingly, the *Orange Bud* (detail shown here) ended up in Fayetteville in the home of one of Bettie Stell's grandsons, when the granddaughter of Mary Elizabeth Harris, the maker, inherited it. Mary Elizabeth pieced it in 1864 in Upson County, Georgia, and she and her Mother quilted it in six weeks. Ary's daughter identified this particular arrangement of the blocks as like that of Talula's. (Photo, NB)

Heavenly Father, boys to help him work it. He set about gathering his crops that fall and picking cotton with the image of Sand Mountain, Alabama, in his mind, and a nice house with stone fireplaces and a big veranda. He prayed to God to keep his wife healthy and give him other sons.

In the middle of the harvest season that fall after Little Johnny died, Tom fell ill with the worst case of malaria he had ever had. The fever attacked him for weeks, and when he began to talk out of his head, Talula was beside herself. She vowed to promise that she would go to Alabama if it would keep him well, but when one night he asked her to send for her father and his brother George to witness his will, she knew he was better, so she never made the promise.

Paying the doctor's bills and the men who had to be hired that fall to harvest the crops absorbed most of the money from the cotton. By January they had only $35 to get them through the winter and start the spring planting, but when a beautiful, healthy baby boy arrived in February, they felt their prayers had been answered. After that great blessing, Tom put away the old *Universalist* books of his father's and began to read and study the Bible for himself. He started with the Old Testament and was amazed at what he found there.

Preparing cloth for the family's needs, c. 1870s.

First, card the cotton (lint cotton); prepare it in little rolls. Next, spin a broach, a spindle full of thread. The broach was on a corn shuck which could be slipped off the spindle. From here it went to the reel, then to the winding blade, then to the cob spools which were on the frames in long rows; some may have used quilting frames for this. Little skinned switches were stuck down through the cob spools. These would put the warp of the cloth on warping frames which were nailed to the kitchen outside Ma's house.

The reel was the thing they wound thread on. When the reel ran off a hundred rounds, it would pop; that was called a cut. About six cuts made a hank. The hank was put on the winding blade, and we would wind the thread off that on to a cob spool which was just a corn cob with the pitch burned out with a burning iron.

The children could help with the spinning by going to the woods to get the dye bark. They would use walnut hulls to dye the woolen thread to make the jeans. It was woolen cloth made strictly of virgin wool. The shirts were always made of coarse, homemade cotton cloth. They wore cotton pants, called copperas pants, dyed with some kind of bark with copperas in the water to set the dye. The little boys all wore copperas pants in the summertime, home woven ones. They never wore drawers in the summer or winter. They just went to bed in their shirt-tails, just took off their coats and pants and went right to bed.

—Thomas J. Bottoms in conversation with
daughter Mollie Ruth in 1940.

CHAPTER 11

On Jordan's Stormy Banks

After the War rural people in Georgia took for granted the necessity to double up families and take in orphans or anyone who needed a home. John Gilbert's family of ten had two hired men always living in the house and often someone else's child. When Holly's sister Jerusha and her husband, Hosea Rogers, both died young leaving two sons, John and Charles, John Gilbert and Analiza took the young Charles and raised him as their own son. The bedrooms were crowded with two or three beds and often pallets—made of folded quilts—on the floor. It is no wonder a bed was a necessary and prominent piece of furniture in the parlor. In addition, Talula remembers, she often got breakfast in the old back kitchen with a hired man sleeping on a cot in the corner. Just as life required no wasted time or energy, there could be no unused inch of space in the house.

Even when someone was gravely ill or dying, no such luxury as a separate room was possible. Quilts were hung up around sick beds to shield the eyes of the sick and suffering from the dead and dying.

Talula could not seem to get well after Walter was born. She had no milk for him, and the black wet nurse they found to live with them also had a little girl of her own in addition to her baby. If her child crossed her in any way "she would tie her apron over her head and take her down in the orchard and beat her terribly," but she had plenty of milk for the two babies. Little Walter thrived, and when he was but six months old Talula found she was pregnant again.

About that time Tom promised a pleading neighbor to take in his twelve-year-old daughter who didn't get along with her

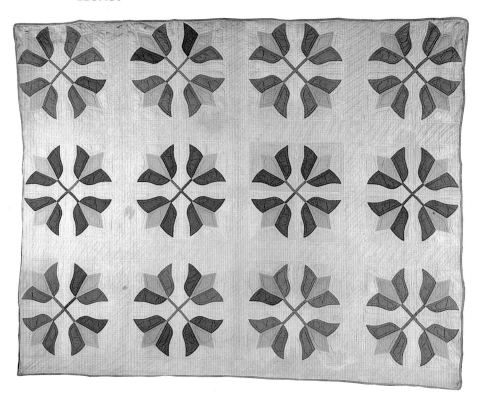

Dutch Tulip, c. 1850s. Probably made by Jerusha [also spelled Jerutia in one source] Murphy Rogers, Talula's aunt and sister of her mother Holly Murphy Gilbert. Both Jerusha and her husband Hosea Rogers "died young" soon after the Civil War, leaving two sons John and Charles who were like brothers to Talula. Perhaps it was because John and Analiza Gilbert raised the young Charles as their own son that he gave this quilt of his mother's to Talula, who was not to receive one of her own mother's quilts. Note attached to quilt, "made by Jerusha Gilbert, Almira's Grandmother," is partly in error. It was probably written long after Talula's death when memory of what she told her daughter was fading, though it is strange Almira would forget that it was Holly who was her grandmother, not Jerusha. Several other articles handmade by Jerusha remain with Talula's descendants.

stepmother. Though the girl seemed sullen and obstinate, Talula thought she could train her to be of some help when the wet nurse left and the new baby came; Talula reluctantly agreed. Talula and Tom began by taking Birdie to meeting with them to get any wild notions out of her head, for Tom was a deacon and Talula had been persuaded to join the Women's Missionary Society devoted to "sending the Gospel to Heathan Lands and the Bible to Earth's remotest Bounds."[1] Talula saw a bit of "the Heathen" in Birdie and thought she should begin at home.

The new baby was another boy. Ary Thomas was born on May Day, 1888, after Elisa had gone back to Alabama for another birth there. Before she left, she warned Tom and Talula to let Birdie go. She saw in the girl an incorrigible streak, but Tom and Talula had promised to give her a home and Talula felt she would be needed when the new baby arrived, even though Birdie disobeyed and once went off with a neighbor boy in defiance of Tom's commands.

That summer began early and was unusually hot. Little Walter died in June of "cholera morbus" despite all the home rem-

Elisa Bottoms's *Throw-Together* quilt, c. 1875–1890, is made of various hand-pieced blocks sewn together for cover during very hard times. The predominant string-pieced, six-point stars in Elisa's quilt utilize every conceivable piece of fabric that could be salvaged from old clothes, as well as scraps of homespun, home-woven material home-dyed in plain colors. The quilt, its backing made with much pieced homespun, is an example of Elisa's incredible frugality and resourcefulness, as well as her natural instinct for order and beauty. The unnamed blocks comprising one border suggest that Talula's characteristic "cross-in-the-center" design of many of her early and later quilts, came from Elisa. (See *Goose Tracks* I, II, III and *Grandmother's Fan*.)

edies and as a last resort, treatment by two doctors, one of whom—Minta's husband, Dr. Edwards—refused the child water despite his high fever, and the other tortured the suffering child with a bowel wash.[2] The child's symptoms had begun when Birdie let him eat a stomach full of cherries off the ground while Talula was "busy making her a pretty white dress" to wear to church. It was too late to blame anyone for Little Walter's death (though they never had either doctor again, and Minta's feelings were hurt), but Tom wanted to send Birdie right back to her father. Talula would not hear of it. She loved the child and would not add to her own grief by rejecting Birdie, who was so full of remorse she went about her work sobbing tears into the food as she cooked.

Before the summer was over, Talula's beloved sister Minta herself was laid to rest not too long after the birth of her first child, and both Nannie Dickson and half-sister Bettie (Stell) had buried their first-born sons.

Talula had diligently taken her two babies to church with Tom, had lifted her heart and her voice to God, and had grieved under the hot sun beside the little graves with her sorrowing sisters; but when Minta died it was as if a great part of

Minta Melvina Gilbert, Talula's "little sister," and husband, Dr. James T. Edwards, *right*. Talula later instructed a photographer to make a bust enlargement of Minta alone. Minta was beautiful, popular, and romantic and was engaged to at least one other man when Dr. Edwards proposed to her. They were married in Fayetteville within a month after she met him and the same day (February 2, 1887) her half-sister Bettie was married to Walter Stell in Jonesboro. Talula was in the last month of pregnancy with Walter and decorum prevented her attendance at either wedding. *Far right:* Talula's half-sister Bettie and husband Walter Stell.

her own life had been torn out. She blamed her own wicked heart for her heavy grief, for her inability to compose even one obituary for all those dear ones gone, and she could not bring herself to seek counsel from the new preacher at Corinth Church. Finally she sat down and poured out her heart in a letter to her much revered former pastor, Rev. A. C. Smith.

In his September 28, 1888, reply to Talula's letter, Reverend Smith wrote, "You said your hope had been strengthened since you began to write and no wonder, for it is always when we do a thing that . . . blesses . . . others . . . we share in the reflex influence upon ourselves."[2] Whether Talula's lifelong habit of writing freely and fluently began at that time or later, it does appear that she learned well the art of letter writing, teaching herself by doing in spite of her lack of education.[3]

That fall Tom had a bad case of malaria again, and before he was completely well he found someone to help him drive the horse and buggy, and left for Alabama. This time he was determined to find a farm that would be a healthy place for himself and his family. But his fever came back when they were halfway there, and he had to return by train and let the other fellow bring his horse and buggy home.

In Tom's absence John Gilbert had decided to give each of his daughters a piece of property. What could Tom do when he learned his father-in-law had deeded the farm that had been his mother's to Talula, had made her an outright gift of it?[4] Once more he swallowed his pride, hoped for better times and better health, and stayed on.

By the time the flu epidemic struck Fayette County in January 1891, Talula and Tom had two healthy little boys, Ary and

An itinerant photographer snapped Tom, Talula and infant Roger in the spring of 1891. Bettie and Minta, Talula's sisters, had fine wedding pictures made, a mark of status. This was Tom and Talula's first picture together. Tom, at age 30, pale and thin from many bouts with malaria, is already losing his hair.

Matt, and baby Roger was just a few weeks old. Tom had built a tenant house on the place where an extra man could live with his family and help him work the farm on shares. He had finally joined in a very small way the great host of farmers across the South who had been forced by the War and Reconstruction into the sharecropper system, a new kind of slavery that would last more than fifty years, until other wars and the era of technology would introduce other economic systems.

When they all had the 'flu, Willie Morris had it too. He was the hired man who lived in the house with them, and his mother came to do the cooking. George Washington Bottoms's daughter Mollie came to wash and iron and help indoors and out wherever needed. Talula's cousin Julia Steele came to nurse the sick folks and empty slop jars.

Elisa had come home from Alabama, and she was the sickest of all. She kept getting out of bed and going to the kitchen door to vomit "to save people trouble" and refused to drink the "lighter'd tea."[5] Talula was too weak, and everyone else too sick or too busy to stop her. With ten people stuffed in the dark, drafty rooms of that old house and seven of them sick, they had to double up in beds as well as rooms. Before they had recovered, Tom, Talula, and the children one by one began to get measles. It was a nightmarish time such as they had not experienced since the War. Almost everyone in the county was sick, and young and old were dying everywhere.

Elisa died January 31, 1891, among her own quilts on the feather bed she had made from her geese. "So many were sick there was hardly anyone to make her a coffin or dig the grave for her. Brother George [her oldest son] and Mr. Simpson dug the grave and buried her right by themselves." Without a funeral the brave and stoic Elisa was thus laid to rest in that lonely graveyard beside her husband.

Mollie stayed until all were over the measles; Julia Steele remained for many weeks until Talula was strong again and "all they ever got out of it was a worsted dress apiece."[6] But Mollie's relationship with her Uncle Tommie's family had been sealed in a bond of devotion that would never be broken.

It must have been soon after that hard winter, when all the quilts were washed and dried in the spring sun, that Talula carefully folded away Elisa's quilts to save for the rest of her life, quilts that would then be passed on to her sons and daughters and to her grandchildren.

LeMoyne Star, c. 1850s or earlier. Made by Holly D. Murphy Gilbert, the "quilt of my mother's" that went to Talula when her brother Matt "died a young man" of tuberculosis in 1889. "A rarer quilt than The Feather . . . made by one of your great-grandmothers . . . a much valued family heirloom," Mollie Ruth wrote to her niece and namesake, Ruth Butler Potts, in March 1966, when she gave the quilt to her with the request she would "pass it on to one of your daughters."

CHAPTER 12

Decision

When Talula received the letter from sister Cathern Allen dunning her for dues as a member of the Women's Missionary Society of Corinth Church, she must have already made peace with her God and herself about her absence from church and the society. "I will say to you this is the Lord's work we are engaged in and the Bible says woe unto the Daughters in Zion who are at ease in another place . . . it is the duty of every Child of God to help in this important work . . . ," Mrs. Allen admonished her.[1] Baby Roger was nine months old, and with little boys two and three and all the house and garden work to do since Elisa's death, Talula was not "at ease in another place." She kept going at a trot all day long, and was bone-tired at night. Neither was she negligent or backsliding; she had decided after Little Walter died not to take her babies out among crowds at the meetings and singings she loved so much but to stay home with her children and try to keep them well. It did not bother her to do the work on Sundays while Tom went to church, for she often leafed through the *Baptist Hymn Book* she had bought so long ago to recall the words of old hymns she loved. She sang as she tended babies, boiled vegetables, and fried chickens for the family and the company that Tom often brought home with him. And it seemed to do her good when she sang the hymns that Elisa loved or ones that Tom's brother Bobbie had sung at her baptizing, to let the tears of joy or grief or longing flow as freely as they liked. How she did miss Mother Elisa, the bravest woman and the nearest thing to a true mother she would ever know! And Bobbie, too, who had died with such a mysterious ailment and whose voice when he led the songs had lifted people almost to the doors of heaven.[2]

Talula remembered the first time Elisa climbed up on the wagon seat beside Tom and went to Alabama to stay with her son James Madison and his wife, to be with Laura when she had her baby. Elisa had decided to divide her quilts among her five children before she left, thinking she might stay there on Sand Mountain with her son Mattie's family. When "Tommy got only the poorest bunch," his mother felt bad and so did Talula, because Tom loved the beautiful *Feather*. But Talula soon overcame her disappointment. She borrowed her sister-in-law Susan's quilt, got material, and made a *Feather* quilt for herself.

It was in the hot summer of 1892 after the birth of their first daughter in July, that Talula's face began to take on a new radiance. It was not only the little red-haired girl sleeping in her cradle beside the big quilting frame that gave her that glow of happiness, but the work itself she was doing. Talula kept her three little boys busy and out of mischief by letting them take turns running in from their play to fan her; she had decided to make time (rather than waiting for it) to do the quilting her hands were itching to do. She put the *Feather* quilt in her frame first.

When at last she took the beautiful *Feather* out of the frame, she could be justly proud of her accomplishment. She had filled it with a thin layer of her own hand-carded cotton that Tom had grown. She had close-quilted it with tiny even stitches that followed the scallops in the big feather plumes. She could hardly wait to put the *Rocky Mountain* in her frame and "quilt it nicely," too. (Talula had learned from Elisa the secret of having good light to work by after the lamps were lit as the October

---

Talula tells Mollie Ruth the history of the *Feather* quilt.

. . . when Mother divided her quilts [1884], Mrs. Liza Elmore was there, and all the daughter-in-laws. So Mrs. Liza placed the quilts, on [five] chairs, as she [Mother] had 5 children, but your Aunt Sarah couldn't be there. So we inlaw's all went into the hall, and Mrs. Liza fixed them as she pleased, and then she let each one say the one she had her hand on was hers. So she had placed the feather quilt on first chair, also other best ones, and next best on second, and so on, until the worst ones were on fifth chair. So naturally oldest one was the one got first chair, next oldest got next best. So Sister Sousan got the Feather quilt and she had two, tho, she had made and quilted them both, but mother paid her for doing all the work. When after all was over and the others had carried their quilts away, mother said to me, that she "did want Tommie to have the Feather quilt," . . . . So Tommie got the very poorest bunch, but they all were good, but just very common quilts. Well I decided I'd get the Feather pattern and make myself one . . .
                                    —Letter, T. Bottoms to M. R. Bottoms, December 11, 1940.

days grew shorter and the dark came on so early. Splinter torches, called "lighter'd," cut from rich pine knots produced a bright flame. Her father had thrown pine knots like that on the fire in winter evenings, and they had blazed up brightly enough for her and her brothers to see while studying. Tom used those same long splinters as torches when he and his hound dog went coon hunting at night.)

When Talula finished quilting those two special quilts, she felt a new and joyful sense of herself. She had developed work habits and quilting skills she was to use as long as she could sit at her frame and quilt. After that, all her best quilts were quilted "by the piece," without using templates or marked patterns of any kind. (The only exception was the earlier *Magnolia Leaf*, done with Elisa's help so soon after her marriage for which she doubtless used little heart stencils to design the love motif for quilting.) Talula simply followed the pieced or appliquéd design, quilting out in as many waved, straight, or angular lines as she pleased. This procedure resulted in a quilting pattern that was uniquely her own, one that changed with every quilt. It was this natural rather than any imposed design that would distinguish her good quilts throughout the rest of her life. In the years that were to follow, the joy she found in that creative and enduring work of her hands would help her rise above untold tribulations. With the eggs, chickens, and butter she herself produced, she could barter in Jonesboro for new material to make as many quilts as her time would allow. Already she had in mind her own children and many others for whom she wanted to make quilts.

It was after their seventh son George was born in 1896 that Talula noticed Tom seemed more troubled and studied his Bible more than usual. Even so she was profoundly shocked when he came home from church one Sunday, pale and shaken, and told her the Baptist Association had voted that Corinth Church must turn him out. Tom had been one of the first to propose that the church must maintain its integrity by disciplining and, if possible, bringing back into the fold any member who strayed, or who by unchristian behavior brought shame to the people of God. He had stood strongly for "turning out" any who refused repentance, had been appointed several times on "committees to investigate" ugly situations—drunkenness, fighting, immoral conduct, making or selling whiskey—but the church, thus far, had not turned out a single member. Some

We had a pretty hard time in raising our large family. We lost three of our ten boys in infantcy and two grown boys after they grew up to be men. Mat was killed accidentally with his own gun after being on a hunting trip and was on his way home. George died in camp of the first world war. We enjoyed our children lots. Had a good time with them when all were well. Sometimes their father would have three or four on his lap at once. Would have two on each knee at a time. And he and the children would enjoy it so much, and I really enjoyed it too, with them.

—Talula Bottoms, Memoir

The Feather, c. 1884–85, quilted, 1892, was Talula's name for this variation of the colonial *Prince's Feather* pattern said to have originated in England, "taken from the crest of the Prince of Wales." This pattern was popular in Fayette County, Georgia, in the late 1800s and was sometimes called *Quincy Feather* by country women there. The two old *Feather* quilts made by Talula's sister-in-law Susan Collins Bottoms, (wife of George Washington Bottoms) as well as her *Rocky Mountain* quilt were inherited by grandchildren and "came all to pieces" when they tried to wash them. (Interview Sarah Bottoms Barber, 1985.) Talula wrote her unmarried daughter Mollie Ruth "the history of the *Feather* quilt" in a letter dated December 11, 1940, soon after she gave this special old quilt to her. The quilt is handmade except for the binding, which is sewn down on top by machine, characteristic of certain 19th-century quilts bound in that manner by women who were first able to afford a treadle sewing machine. Talula's first treadle sewing machine was bought in 1895. Her last (a 1920s model) was found in Tennessee in 1987.

Detail of *The Feather.*

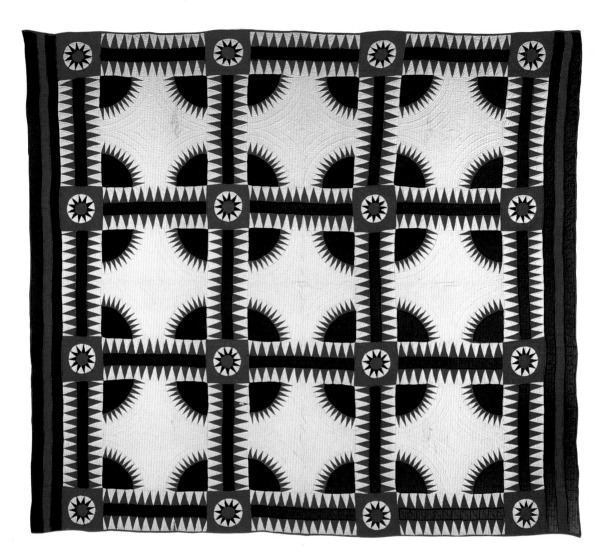

Rocky Mountain, above, c. 1883, quilted 1892 or 1893. This was Talula's name for the popular nineteenth century quilt—later called the *New York Beauty*—that Talula borrowed to get the pattern from "Aunt Mollie," her stepmother's sister, later to be her father's third wife. The quilt was "Papa's favorite," admired by all who saw it and chosen in the early 1940s by at least one of Talula's granddaughters as the one she wanted. Since it had been promised to her daughter Almira, Talula began another that was incomplete at her death in 1946. This prompted that granddaughter, who inherited much of Talula's unfinished work, to make her own *Rocky Mountain* in 1986. Talula's *Rocky Mountain* is completely handmade except for the top stitching of the binding, as are four others of her best quilts. *Left:* Detail of *Rocky Mountain.*

I had to quit taking my babies out to any gathering of any kind, because it made them sick to carry them to a gathering. Then I had them stay well, and reared them. So I staid at home with my little ones.
—Talula Bottoms, Memoir

had fallen away by their own choice and had been removed from membership, but everyone knew there was no more God-fearing man in Fayette County than Tom Bottoms.

The commotion had begun the day he brought before the church the several ways he believed they were going against the laws of God, and acknowledged he had been keeping the seventh day of the week as the Sabbath and aimed to continue obeying the fourth commandment.[3] Corinth Church people knew this man to be above reproach, "his life a sermon wherever he walked,"[4] and they were willing to allow him that deviation from church doctrine as long as he kept regular attendance and didn't voice his queer views about too much. He was merely an embarrassment to them. But Tom was not a man to keep his firm convictions to himself. He felt it his duty to set his fellow Christians straight, and the Association was firm in its determination to turn him out. It grieved Talula to the depths of her soul to see him do it, but Tom soon asked for his church letter and removed himself from the sacred rolls of those people of God, though he continued faithfully to attend meetings and take his sons to church. Nevertheless, it saddened him that his fellow Christians did not realize the error of their ways, and it made more solid his decision to move to Alabama.

CHAPTER 13

Upheaval

ayette County was born out of the violence and bloodshed of the Creek Indian War in Georgia, and the people who lived there knew about the blood sacrifice made by Chief William McIntosh when he signed over the White Sticks tribal lands to the state of Georgia in 1825. It is doubtful, however, if many of the "Georgia Crackers" who migrated to Sand Mountain in Alabama after the Civil War knew the little town of Logan was named for a man who had assisted General Sherman in the violence and bloodshed that left Atlanta in ruins and Georgia a wasteland. Like many another Yankee soldier, Bob Freeman, who fought under Union Major General John Alexander Logan, was impressed with the lush beauty and protective mountains of North Alabama as his regiment marched from Vicksburg to Georgia in 1864. When he returned to that area after the War, it was he who named the remote settlement on Brindley Mountain for General Logan.[1]

In November 1898 Tom travelled again to Sand Mountain, went to the little hamlet of Logan, and put down $600 he had secretly saved on a $900 farm of "160 acres with a nice house and enough land cleared to make a crop."[2] (In 1884 he could have had the same land as a homesteader for $18 and his promise to remain there for at least three years.) He went home then to finish gathering his crops, sell his cotton, arrange to rent out the Fayette County farm with its two houses, and plan for the difficult journey. Mr. Jim Pierce, Tom's friend and sharecropper, and Jim's family, would go ahead in December in two covered wagons driving cows and mules and taking household goods. Tom and Talula and their seven children would follow in January by train.

With six children ages two to ten and an infant not six weeks old, Talula accepted as routine that the Pierce family would live with them for a time. She took for granted, too, the "nice

The Rev. T. J. Bottoms, *below.* Tom had strongly felt "the call to preach" in the 1890s. After Tom received a discouraging reply to his letter soliciting Association support from the Rev. A. C. Smith in 1895, the church at Corinth ordained him. It was then he began to "search the scriptures" for his own understanding of the truths they held that changed the course of his (and his family's) life forever.

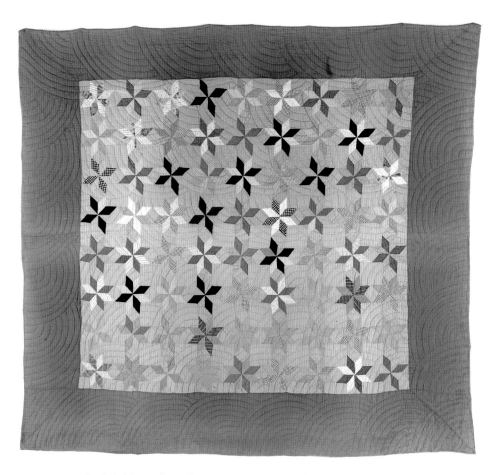

Little LeMoyne Star, above, c. 1890–1920. One of two scrap quilts (the other was an *Autumn Leaf*) used for every day by daughter Almira and washed many times. Both may have been made by Talula during the Cullman County years.

house" would be unpainted, weatherbeaten, and set precariously on flat stones at the corners, but she did not know it would have a windy dog trot running between the two main rooms straight through to the back yard, nor how small and inconvenient it would be for two families numbering fourteen people. Neither did she realize they would have to live all jammed together for three years in that little house.

"Will adjust to whatever happens, will not worry. If a thing can be helped I will help it; if not I will make the best of it," had been her resolve as a girl, and this move would require every emotional and physical resource she could muster. Nonetheless, she cried all the time she was getting ready to go. As she wrote her Memoir forty-three years later, she was still profoundly moved by the memory:

> It grieved me very much to have to leave our childhood home, country, and the old home we both loved so well, and my father, and he had bought the old Bottoms home to keep us there. It surely was heartbreaking, tho I did not back out . . . for I thought it might keep us from having so much malaria. . . .

Cullman County had been aggressively promoted as a healthy and potentially prosperous area by a German immigrant, Colonel Johann G. Cullman. Unlike Talula's memory of Fayette County where "everyone was on equality and loved

Excerpt from Talula's Memoir.

91

gather his crop and arrange to move to Alabama. It grieved me very much to have to leave our childhood home, country, and the old home that we both loved so well, and my old Father, and he had bought the old Bottoms home to keep us there. It surely was heart breaking bad me to have to leave there. Tho I did not back out moving to Alabama. for I that it might be a help to keep us from so much malaria fever. So me went to work geting ready to move as soon as we could. Tho we didn't get to leave there until until Burlie was 6 weeks old. That was in February, as he was born 11 day December

92

1898. So me carried him to ala. and Mr. Jim Pierce & family had already gone out there and carried the wagon and teem for us, and a few things in wagon. and they had to have a house built for them to live in on the place. So they didn't have the house finished when we got there. So we all had to live there together in the same house until they could finish the house. and the girls seemed to love the baby, Burlie as if he'd been their own brother. So we all got him spoiled, and he wanted to be rocked in the little baby crib that we brot from Georgia and it may made by an uncle

Tom Bottoms's birthplace, the old James Bottoms home in Fayette County, Georgia (c. 1840) was Talula and Tom's first home. Talula gave birth to nine children in that house and by daylight, lamplight, and "lightered" made a dozen or more quilts. Talula would not have the old ivy-covered tree cut down, for the birds loved it and their singing entertained her babies when she would put them on a pallet on the porch.

each other," the area consisted largely of two distinct groups: enterprising, competitive, and better educated German immigrants who were building fine homes in and around the town of Cullman, and "poor dirt farmers" from Georgia and other southern states who occupied the wooded hill country. The farm families could barely eke out a living until they had cleared and "cleaned" the land by burning and grubbing out the root system so it could be plowed to grow cotton, sweet potatoes, and other cash crops. Nevertheless, Tom Bottoms at thirty-nine finally had his own land; he was accustomed to hard work, and his enthusiasm knew no bounds. With three sons old enough to be taught and three more coming along, as well as Jim Pierce and his grown son to help, Tom set to work clearing the land with a vengeance. He did not have malaria anymore; he soon learned there was no Alabama law against working on Sunday, and he began to look around for other "Sabbath keepers." Surprisingly, he found a little group of people about sixty-five miles east at Attalla. It was a difficult two-day trip, but in his zeal for the truth, Tom began travelling there occasionally to preach and attend Sabbath Day services.

Back in Georgia people were prosecuted for working on Sunday, and Tom had been frustrated trying to farm with only five days a week to work, for he obeyed to the letter the fourth commandment and still went to church with his sons on preaching days at Corinth. He had asked Talula then if she "aimed to keep the Sabbath" with him, and she was quick to respond: "I told him no, that I couldn't keep two days as many children and as much work as I had to do . . . that I should work 7 days a week instead of 5. . . ."[3]

For Talula (and Tom's niece Mollie back in Georgia) the upheaval of the move was wrenching. "When Mr. Jack came in his wagon to take you I felt just like the hearse had come seeing you all fixing to go . . . the poor little younguns . . ." The children were bright-eyed and eager to leave, but on the long, unaccustomed journey by train all grew weary and restless and two became so sick they kept throwing up before Talula could get to the restroom with them. Thus the whole family arrived finally at Cullman station with soiled clothes and smelling of vomit, emotionally drained, and exhausted.

Tom, Talula, and the baby rode ahead with Mr. Carter King in his buggy to the farm. The children followed with Mr. Pierce in an open wagon. An icy wind whipped through their clothes, and the cold darkness fell upon them before the slow, jolting ride brought the children the ten interminable miles up and down steep hills, across creeks and ravines to their strange new home. They were chilled to the bone; little George cried and screamed as if he had been delivered to the gates of hell, and Talula could do nothing to stop him until he fell exhausted to sleep. For many days he awoke in the morning crying heart-brokenly as if he had been utterly betrayed.

No sooner had they begun to thaw out and unpack than a rare, heavy blizzard blew furiously across Sand Mountain bringing a record freeze. The two families had to eat, sleep, and cook with all fourteen people huddled about the old fireplace in the kitchen to keep warm.

As soon as the snow melted, Tom made the all-day journey to Cullman, sloshing and bumping over deep ruts and muddy ravines, the dirt roads still partially frozen, and bought Talula a new cast-iron stove. How proud she was of that handsome convenience! It would warm up the kitchen so fast and save her so much bending and heavy lifting, so much scorching of her face and hands while her back shivered from the cold! And how wonderful to have the new set of pots and skillets that came as a bonus with the stove. Those were the first new cooking utensils Talula ever had, for she had used Elisa's heavy blackened pots ever since her marriage. Buying that stove was the first of many tangible ways Tom would try to make life easier for his wife. She had already borne nine children, was still only thirty-seven years old, and before the year was out she would be pregnant again.

The blizzard hit Fayette County with even greater fury. Mollie sent a complete report of "what people around here done to keep their stock and things from freezing" in the first of several hundreds of letters she would write over the ensuing years to her Aunt Lula. "The chickens' combs all froze. The Guineas feet froze and I'm afraid they will all come off. They are rising but we caught them and greased them with lard and gunpowder as it says in Dr. Chase's book but I'm afraid it will do no good they don't potrack any hardly. Lots of folks have lost all their Guineas. Our fruit froze in the jars . . . our eggs froze and burst. Mrs. Camp said her eggs burst within six feet of the fire . . . Mr. Gibson put his calf in the shuckhouse and Mr. Farmer put his in the corn crib. Mrs. Ellis turned her cow and calf together in the stall and hung up quilts around them and the horses. . . ." Mr. Rosenbloom, the peddler, had just been around and "bought 100 dozen eggs" from farm people to sell in Atlanta, "but he got shet of them by hard work and lots of walking. 'So a peddler has a hard life, hey,' he says. . . . Pa tied up his feet and went out and picked a basketful of (cotton) bolls and we are pulling it out right here in the house . . . it sure is hard work. The boys said he would freeze, but Pa said he could do that as well as they could rabbit hunt. . . ."4

When the hard freeze in Georgia gave way to a sea of mud and slush in March, Mollie wrote that her father had to buy two loads of sand for their yard before they could even get out to the mail box without miring knee-deep in the sticky stuff. Then Talula was glad of the natural dark sand of their own bare yard on Brindley Mountain.

It was the picture Mollie sent with her March 10 letter of their old home in Fayette County that awakened in Talula and the children a homesickness so deep she had to put the photograph away. It opened up a well of tears for little George again, and five-year-old Emmett's pleading to go home wrung Talula's heart. The old bird tree outside the kitchen window dominated the picture, and part of the house did not show; but that image of home with all its familiar symbols of love and security, joy of family and friends, bird songs and farm sounds was too much for Talula and her children. She tucked it away and kept the children busy with routine tasks.

Mollie's letters came regularly and kept Talula closely in touch with every loved detail of life back home in Georgia, while she and Tom seemed to be starting all over again as pioneers. She must have thought often of her grandmother Tab-

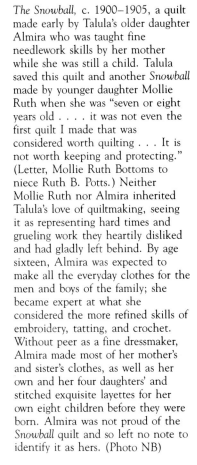

The Snowball, c. 1900–1905, a quilt made early by Talula's older daughter Almira who was taught fine needlework skills by her mother while she was still a child. Talula saved this quilt and another *Snowball* made by younger daughter Mollie Ruth when she was "seven or eight years old . . . . it was not even the first quilt I made that was considered worth quilting . . . It is not worth keeping and protecting." (Letter, Mollie Ruth Bottoms to niece Ruth B. Potts.) Neither Mollie Ruth nor Almira inherited Talula's love of quiltmaking, seeing it as representing hard times and grueling work they heartily disliked and had gladly left behind. By age sixteen, Almira was expected to make all the everyday clothes for the men and boys of the family; she became expert at what she considered the more refined skills of embroidery, tatting, and crochet. Without peer as a fine dressmaker, Almira made most of her mother's and sister's clothes, as well as her own and her four daughters' and stitched exquisite layettes for her own eight children before they were born. Almira was not proud of the *Snowball* quilt and so left no note to identify it as hers. (Photo NB)

Old Walker Schoolhouse, Cullman County Alabama, c. 1906. It was built by Thomas Jefferson and James Madison Bottoms with help of their nephews James Franklin and George Washington Walker and other neighbors on property donated by several neighboring farmers near the site of the first log schoolhouse Tom and Matt Bottoms built on Tom's property across Lick Creek. The crumbling well house, later used as a barn, still stands overrun by brush and trees near the pile of rotting boards that was once the country school. Mr. Willie Tillery was the teacher when this picture was taken. George Daniel Bottoms is in the doorway looking back.

Jonesboro Ga.
Apr. 12th 1899.

Dear Allie I will write you a
short letter I was very glad
to read your little letter
I want to see you so bad
I will send you a scrap to
go in your little bed quilt
you must kiss little Barrel
and George for me, nothing
more at present you must
write again Yours Lovingly

Ozelie

Mollie's letter to Almira Bottoms,
age six.

itha and told her own children the stories of the Georgia wilderness she had been told as a child. On that remote wooded farm between Lick Creek and Crooked Creek they were more than ten miles from Cullman and not a sound came from the sleepy little hamlet of Logan two miles to the east. Back in Fayette County they could hear the train whistle blow, the courthouse clock strike the hours, and the big iron school bells toll the time for books. Here there was no school and not a sound at night except the lonely lowing of cattle or barking of dogs.

One night at supper when Tom had gone off to Attalla, Talula was quite beside herself with the children's quarreling. Exasperated, she told them if they didn't quiet down some animal would come and get them, for panthers, wildcats, and wild hogs were said to roam the woods. She had hardly spoken when the dog set up a furious barking and a heavy thud struck the kitchen door. The children fell suddenly silent, frozen in fear, for a scratching of heavy claws shook and rattled the door.

Talula fastened the wooden latch and hustled the scared children off to bed, herself frightened almost to death. Next morning they found great marks scarring the kitchen door and big tracks in the yard. Their old hound dog was cowering under the house.

When Talula learned there was no school anywhere around for her children to attend, and in spite of her own limited education, she got out the old readers and arithmetic books and "held a little school there at the house" for her own, the young Pierces, and several other children. Some parents insisted on paying "tuition"; they had no money so they paid in chickens or eggs or pigs.[5]

One of the lessons Talula devised for her classes, "just like they would have been held in a regular school," was to set the children writing letters back home to Georgia. Among the hundreds of letters Talula saved were the pleased replies to her pupils' childish letters. One of them indicates Talula was already teaching her six-year-old daughter Almira to sew.

One or another of the children had been sick ever since the move; when spring came, Talula herself collapsed and went to bed. Tom and his brother, with the neighbors' help, then built a log schoolhouse on the Logan road across Lick Creek and found a teacher.[6] They cut down a tree and let it fall across the creek for a foot bridge for the children. Only once or twice did a child fall off that big log into the creek on the way to school.

CHAPTER 14

Return and Farewell

It was a proud moment when Tom and Talula were able to send back to their families in Georgia the big picture of their greatly enlarged and newly painted Cullman County home. Before their first year was out, they had enclosed the dog trot for an entrance hall, cut two large windows for sleeping rooms in the loft, and replaced the old ladder leading to them with an enclosed stairway. By 1905 they had added a new dining-room wing on the back and built a fine new fireplace of sandstone and limestone hauled up from Lick and Crooked creeks. Tom and his sons had designed and built an elegant front veranda with Victorian trim, and a convenient side porch near a new hand-dug well for the water bucket and wash pan. Finally, they had built a ladder long enough to reach to the top of the four proud gables and had painted the house a light gray with brilliant white trim. Except for a little front balcony, Tom thought this wonder he and his sons had wrought looked as fine as Miss Mayme Fitzgerald's Rural Home across Flint River back in Georgia.

When they had all dressed in their best clothes, most of them made by Talula herself, the photographer came from Cullman, posed them all on the veranda, and took their pictures. For Tom that symbol of his success must have justified the move that had been so wrenching for his dear wife, and yet so essential for himself.

Talula was proud, too, of what her husband and her oldest sons had achieved, though her heart often ached to see how hard they all had to work—from before dawn until after dark, yet she marveled at the way Tom managed to make the work seem like play to his sons. He would set up contests and races to see who could hoe the best row of corn or pick the most cotton. They would all come in for dinner, dust-covered and sweating, and jostle each other for a turn at the dipper and wash pan on

T. J. Bottoms family on veranda of their first "painted" home, near Logan in Cullman County, Alabama, c. 1905. Left to Right: Ary, Maude Pierce, Maude Walker, Emmett, George and Burrell (on edge of porch), Matt, Tom, Mollie Ruth, Gilbert, Talula, Almira, Roger.

the side porch. The noon mealtime would be filled with their congratulations and bragging "to beat you all this evenin."

They had cleared crop land and pastures for milk cows and beef cattle, planted and harvested respectable crops of cotton and corn, and set out a bountiful orchard and vineyard that, together with Talula's garden, provided all the fruit and vegetables they could eat and more. They had built barns and a milk house while the Pierces were still living with them; now the Pierce family had their own home and had vacated the tenant house for another family of hard-working farmers. Talula did so wish her good old father could see how well Tom was doing now on his own land at last. She was as proud as Tom to send that fine picture of her home and family for her father, sisters, and brothers to see.

Talula had never ceased to feel keenly the separation from her people, and she longed to see them again. Her father had just written ". . . as I am the oldest white man in Jonesboro I feel my time is getting very short for this life. . . ." She had not been to see him for what seemed a very long time, and now she had another son to show him, two-year-old Gilbert Aaron, her eleventh child, born just before Christmas 1903.

Her first Alabama child, a second daughter, had arrived in September 1901. In December of that year, Cousin Maude Walker had written from Birmingham that the railroad was

Carpenter's Wheel, c. late 1800s, has also been called *Star with Diamonds* and *Dutch Rose.* Talula's *Carpenter's Wheel* spent four months at Battle Creek Sanitarium in Michigan while she was recuperating from almost-fatal surgery. It narrowly escaped being sold (to help cover expenses, or just because another patient "fell in love" with it). When in the mid-thirties the quilt travelled back to Michigan as a gift to Talula's son Gilbert and his wife Mayme, Mollie Ruth's feelings were hurt. Almira had her heart set on the quilt, too; so Talula proceeded to make two other quilts by this pattern. She hired someone to quilt the one she gave Mollie Ruth. The other seems to have been given to Almira with many other unquilted tops in the 1940s. (Interview, Gilbert and Mayme Bottoms, October 1985, and letter Mayme Bottoms to Ruth B. Potts, 1981.)

The quilt appears to have been pieced in the 1880s and quilted in the 1890s, for it is entirely handmade except for the narrow binding sewn by machine to the homespun backing, then turned over the front and stitched down with black thread, as if to emphasize that feature of the quilt. The imperfections in the backing suggest it was woven by Elisa Bottoms on the old loom Tom described so vividly, probably in the 1870s or 1880s. (Conversation with Merikay Waldvogel, April 1987.)

merchandising a "Holiday Excursion Plan" for family travel. Tom still had the harvest to complete, but Talula thought how wonderful it would be if she could manage alone to take her baby, Mollie Ruth, and the four youngest children, ages three to nine, to visit her family. She and Tom had just finished paying the debt on their farm, and Tom had promised her a visit home then.

They left the day after Christmas, Talula little dreaming of the nightmare such travel would be. The railroad had coupled on eleven extra cars to accommodate the happy holiday crowds, and all became a melee of angry pushing, shoving, fainting—children crying, getting sick, and vomiting. The old engine rebelled, and the train was four hours late to Atlanta where her brother Joe was to meet her.

No one knows how much damage was done to the body of that small woman "looking out for self and chaps and satchel and grip," as she carried the heavy load alone, changed trains in Birmingham, was directed the wrong way "right between two trains, then had to walk as far back the other way" and almost collapsed. When her brother Joe failed to meet her, she was forced to hunt for a hotel in Atlanta.

"Tell Maude," she wrote Tom later, "she need not never name excursion to me again, for it is not the way I want to travel. . . . If you'd known how it was you wouldn't have let me come and if I had known I would have been at home right now. . . ."[1]

She did endure, however, and within two days after their arrival at her father's house, they had all recovered. No less than forty sisters and brothers, cousins and friends, and their families had come to welcome her, to embrace her and her five wonderful children, and to shed tears of joy with her for this glad reunion. Quilts were brought out and pallets made on the floor for callers and their children, for some could not bear to leave but wanted to stay and talk far into the night. When all were sleeping, Talula sat down and wrote a vivid account of her trip to Tom. Already she was longing to see him again, as well as their three sons left at home to help their father pick the last of the cotton.

When in January 1906 John Gilbert again wrote to his daughter, "All well except Myself, I have a terrible itching umer in my blood, it terrifies me sometimes . . . though I will crawl out again like a lizzard when the sun shines . . . ," Talula began immediately to prepare to go to Georgia with Tom. Even as

Talula sitting proudly beside Tom in the little, old-fashioned buggy they took to many an all-day-singing-and dinner-on-the-ground while they lived in Cullman County.

plans were being made, Talula came down with flu and could not seem to get over it. When Tom got sick, too, their twelve-year-old daughter was left with all the housework, cooking, and waiting on sick parents, able to attend school only in snatches. Talula knew it was wrong to go and leave "sister" with all that work.

But when Talula's sister Nannie wrote in June "I went to see Pa last week. He has been very feeble and was fixing to go to Indian Springs to stay awhile," Talula was alarmed and felt she must go to see her "good old father" once more. She could not bear the thought of never seeing him again; she knew he would not go to be treated by the doctors at that expensive place, except as a last resort. Indian Springs was a health center southeast of Atlanta in what is now Butts County, a long buggy-ride from Fayetteville, where in 1821 the Treaty of Indian Springs had been signed with Creek Indian Chief William McIntosh ceding "White Sticks" tribal lands to the state of Georgia. It was believed that drinking from the sulphur springs there would prolong life and restore health, even of desperately ill people.

Talula waited and hoped she would feel well enough to make the trip to Jonesboro, but it seemed as if she never would be strong again. In July when Tom's brother Mattie brought the message from G. E. Deemer who had one of only two telephones in the community of Logan, Talula still was not well and Tom went alone to spend his father-in-law's last hours with him.

Honey Bee, right, and *Star of Bethlehem, below,* c. 1890–1910. Though both of these quilts express Talula's love of red, green, and white for her "nice" quilts, it is the unstable blue-green in these two that suggest they were made about the same time. It is also the fine white fabric (resembling percale), the eye-measured cross hatch quilting, and the narrow Turkey red binding that has been attached to front of both quilts by sewing machine and expertly hand whipped down on the backs. The backing in both quilts is unbleached muslin, and the blocks of both have been joined quite skillfully by sewing machine. In both quilts the blue-green tends to fade toward a brownish hue hardly noticeable in the *Honey Bee,* which has never been washed and rarely exposed to light. The *Star of Bethlehem* was used on best beds for a number of years, and the fading and a few stains *make it look older. (Honey Bee* photo by NB)

It was Nannie who had nursed her father for weeks, had witnessed his suffering, and who had sent to Talula her father's last words, "If this is death it sure is sweet." After that Nannie wrote with more urgency to Talula pleading for her sister's return to Georgia. She wrote less frequently when little more than two years later her son William was killed under the wheels of the train right in front of her house. Her letters then cried out in loneliness and heartache to her sister, younger but so much stronger and more fortunate, she felt, than herself.

"Mrs. Lula Bottoms, My Darling," Tom began in the brief letter he wrote to her after her father died. Talula got up from her sick bed long enough to pour out her grief to him in a long letter in which she also urged him to stay on to visit friends and relatives in Fayetteville and Jonesboro "as long as you want." But it was Mollie's letter that she read and read again as she shared the vivid details of her father's funeral with her children, allowing them to join in her mourning: the crowds of people, the many flowers, the tears that were shed as the mourners moved sorrowfully past the open casket and sang, "God be with you 'till we meet again."[2]

After that Talula began to feel "stouter" and started to "take care of all the fruit that is ready." The next two letters she wrote to Tom while he was away report, among other things, that she had put up ninety-three cans of fruit, cut and dried all the apples, and "kept Sister [Almira] and Emmett home one day to help me wash." One ends with a P.S. "I suppose that boy that got shot is dead by now. The last we heard his brains was running out." The young Limestone County boy had run away from home, had "loaded a gun too heavy and the barrel bursted."

Detail of *Star of Bethlehem.*

Talula wrote matter-of-factly about incidents like that tragic accident. Her letters reveal a woman intensely aware and interested in the life process, wherever and however it occurred; her descriptions spell out every sad or happy or shocking occurrence. Her innocent and uninhibited expression seemed to grow naturally out of deep and compassionate feelings as she learned to accept the reality of "Life and death upon one tether/ and running beautiful together."[3] Before the next year rolled around she would be pregnant with her twelfth child.

The son who was born in August 1907 lived only a year. Although Talula had been as proud as a new mother of Jessie, this tenth son, and considered him a blessing from God, she was forty-five, and her health declined rapidly after his birth. "Sister" was fifteen; and since no other help could be found or afforded, she took over much of her mother's work, taking care of the baby and becoming nurse to both. She lost the whole fall term from school that year and began to study at home to take the state teacher's exam.

The year before, Talula's half-sister Bettie had given birth to twins in Fayetteville. They were her ninth and tenth children, and she was glad one of them was a girl. Though Bettie had "married well" into one of the finest old families in Fayette County, she was as heavy laden as Talula with gardening, sewing, raising chickens, cleaning, washing, and ironing for her family. It was after Jessie's birth that Bettie had written to her sister: "Lula, I was indeed sorry your baby was not a girl for help seems so scarce out there, and I'm sure you need all the help you can get as well as I do, but I keep a negro girl and guess I'll get me a cook this evening—I keep two, one to help with the babies and one to cook. . . ."[4]

Talula dearly loved her half-sister Bettie, and this perhaps unintentional reminder that Talula's marriage was less desirable than her own did not daunt her, nor did she regret this new child was a boy, knowing an all-wise God had sent him. There was never in Talula's attitude or conduct a hint that she felt anything but pride and good fortune in her many sons and in her choice of husband, even though her life in Cullman County had been hard. The record left of those years is sketchy, but one thing stands out clearly in Tom's and Talula's letters from that time: their absolute devotion to each other. Despite the hardships, theirs was "a perfect marriage," as their daughters called it after their parents were gone. "Tell Uncle Tommie," Mollie replied to her aunt's letter on Talula's forty-fourth wedding anniversary, "I was satisfied you all was still in love, for I had never heard of any crosses in all these years. . . ."[5]

What is apparent in other saved letters, though not in Talula's Memoir, is that neither she nor Tom was ever satisfied on the Cullman County farm. At least a dozen letters replying to their inquiries refer to specific farms in Georgia, southern Alabama, and four other states where they might find land more conducive to profitable farming. Six letters bear 1906 dates, suggesting they had already recognized the limitations of the thin sandy soil for farming profitably. Frequent and persuasive notes came from friends and relatives in Georgia reporting this or that place for sale and pleading with them to "come home." Various letters indicate it might indeed have been Talula's choice to return to Georgia, while Tom was diligently looking elsewhere, so there was a tension between Tom and Talula as well as mutual dissatisfaction in Cullman. Yet for fifteen years they made no move.

The older children grew up and began to earn a little money by teaching in country schools; they entertained relatives and friends, cousins from Georgia. Claude Bottoms came and held a singing school, and the house rang with young voices as nine extra young people stayed at their house for three weeks; they bought an organ for their daughters and had great singings.

Tom and Talula Bottoms family picture, c. 1908, in Cullman County after the death of twelfth child, Jesse. The family custom of having a group picture made after a funeral underscores Talula's recognition of the brevity and preciousness of life. Standing left to right: Emmett, Roger, Almira, Ary. Middle row: Brother Leath (a minister who lived with the family for a while), Mollie Ruth, Talula, Tom. Seated: Burlie, Gilbert, George.

Log Cabin, c. late 1800s. The dyes used in most of the green fabric of this old quilt began early to fade through use and washing though Talula carefully preserved it and gave it before her death to her daughter-in-law Alice. It was later inherited by one of Talula's great granddaughters who, unaware of its value, used it for years with children and dogs in her van and on picnics. When recently it was found in Michigan, it proved to be a close mate to the *Carpenter's Wheel,* made entirely by hand in just the same manner, with the same kind of homespun lining. Talula's close quilting of the "logs" has preserved the cotton almost intact, even though most of the red fabric has completely disintegrated from hard use and many machine washings. (Photo NB)

Tom and Talula rejoiced when one by one their children began to confess their faith and join the church. Some of them went to the Emeus Baptist Church Tom's brother James Madison had founded near his farm north of Logan; Talula and Tom hitched up their best horse to the little old-fashioned buggy and went to all-day singings at the Methodist Church on Fifth Sunday in Logan. They rested on the Sabbath Day, and Tom held worship for his family at home when he did not saddle his horse on Thursday and take two days to ride the sixty-five miles to Attalla for Sabbath services there on Saturday.

Tom felt it no sacrifice to make that long journey on horseback. He could arrive at his cousin's house before sundown on Friday, for it was then, according to the scriptures, the Sabbath began. It troubled him but little that his grown children seemed more drawn to the Sunday churches, and that Talula felt she just couldn't spare the time to make the long trip with him to Attalla. He knew eventually they would all see the truth and obey it.

One dark day in March would test the power of Tom's faith and make his children stand in awe of their father's God-centered life. That day may have been the turning point in drawing Talula closer to her husband's firm beliefs. The weather had been unseasonably warm for February and a storm was threatening when Tom hurried in from the field in mid-afternoon, driven by lashing gusts of wind and heavy raindrops. He called Talula and the children together, and they all stood and watched the black cloud approach over the ridge of Brindley Mountain from the southwest. Swirling and rising above the trees, it trailed the dreaded dark funnel; in a continuous roar of thunder and whipping rain it headed straight toward the house. The younger children, like frightened chicks looking for shelter, clung to Talula's skirts; and the older ones, terrified, looked to their father and tried to pray. Only Tom was calm. He looked straight into the storm and in his firm voice admonished his family not to fear but to pray with him that this thing would spare their home and themselves. Almost before he spoke, the funnel cloud divided and the two black tails went roaring and thrashing by Tom Bottoms's farm, tearing up trees a half-mile away on either side and shaking the house until the windows rattled. But the house stood firm, and the humble family relaxed in silent wonder; a miracle had passed before their eyes.

In 1909 Tom had organized a little Sabbath church with seven members that met in Walker Schoolhouse, and two of his sons had joined. By 1912 it had grown to twenty, brother Mattie's family making up a large part of the congregation. Talula had become increasingly ashamed of taking her sewing or knitting out of Tom's sight on Saturdays and joined Tom and her family in this Sabbath worship. "Then all our family kept the Sabbath day," Talula wrote years later, remembering the good things that happened in Cullman County. But there was much she did not write about in her *Memoir*. She does not mention her own ill health, her suffering, her miscarriage; nor does she tell about the tornado that spared their family, though she told the story of that miracle to her grandchildren as, indeed, their parents told and re-told it to their children's great wonder and delight.

Talula had taken with her from Georgia an almanac with a notation about the best time to set duck eggs and had begun developing a flock soon after the family was settled. By 1910 she was raising prize ducks and selling setting eggs to others, packing and shipping them as far away as Milledgeville, Georgia. An undated clipping from the *Atlanta Journal* prints a letter from Mrs. T. J. Bottoms of Logan, Alabama, inquiring about a market for young Indian Runner ducks as broilers. A reply by Loring Brown, Poultry Editor, suggests "clubs and first-class hotels in Atlanta." Talula also saved clippings and inquiries regarding her Buff Orphington and White Plymouth rock chickens which she had become expert at raising. Thus Talula had developed a small independence despite her ill health; and when she could do little else, she sat and pieced quilts. She and Mollie "talked" quilts in their letters and exchanged scraps of cloth. How many quilts came from her busy hands during those years may never be known, but with nine children and some almost old enough for marriage, she was surely making quilts for all of them to take someday to their new homes.

By spring 1913 Talula was so ill with "female problems" it became obvious that some special attention must be paid to her health if she were to live. Tom and Talula's experience with medical doctors had justifiably made them distrustful. Tom was unwilling to take Talula to one of the doctors in Cullman, for they were strangers, and the couple had exhausted their efforts with folk and patent medicines. Then there was the delicacy of her particular condition; it would have bordered on sin for Tom to have a man examine his wife. Second son Matt had gone to Battle Creek Sanitarium in Michigan for his own health in 1909, and by 1913 he was ready to enter training to become a doctor. Third son Roger was also at Battle Creek, working at the Sanitarium and going to high school. Matt at age twenty-

Talula Bottoms with unidentified nurse at Battle Creek Sanitarium in Michigan, 1913. Her surgery and treatment there were paid for in bales of cotton which ironically were lost when the warehouse in Battle Creek where they were stored burned before they could be sold. Talula at age 51 travelled alone by train to Michigan at the end of March, frail and suffering from "female problems." After surgery and four months of therapy, she came home, rested if not well, and immediately began to prepare for the upheaval of another move—this one 60 miles north to a farm three miles west of Athens, Alabama.

Full-Blown Tulip. This old pieced pattern (c. 1800–1825 according to Orlafsky's *Quilts in America*) with its curved patches was considered "next to impossible" to piece and maintain square blocks by Ruth Finley in *Old Patchwork Quilts.* "Only a soul in desperate need of nervous outlet" she says, could execute such a pattern. Made between 1900 and 1920, probably in Cullman County, Talula's quilt is perfectly executed, the blocks pieced by hand. The quilt had never been washed until 1986 when it came through with no fading and only minor shrinkage.

three had become as diligent and articulate as his mother in writing letters to his family, and as responsible in his concern for their welfare. It was he who persuaded his mother to seek treatment in Michigan at the end of March 1913.

Tom was busy with the urgent work of planting cotton; times were hard, and he could scrape up money for train fare only by selling a milk cow and her new calf. Though Tom was greatly alarmed, he left work on the farm to his sons for only a day to get his frail, suffering wife to the train station in Cullman so she could make the long day-coach journey to Battle Creek alone. There her son Matt persuaded Dr. Harvey Kellogg, head of the sanitarium, to accept payment for Talula's treatment in bales of cotton. Talula underwent an operation, but it could not have been very successful for this woman who had waited too long after bearing all those children and doing so much heavy work.

CHAPTER 15

Broken Circles

When Talula returned from her four months at Battle Creek, health improved and face glowing from good nutrition, rest, and attention, she took from her satchel two folded sheets of sanitarium stationery and gave them to Tom. She had finally "got her consent" to move again and had written a vivid description of their farm to advertise its sale. The ad underscored what must have been superhuman effort to carve out that little estate with its "9-room dwelling, 3 stone fireplaces, 2 good tenant houses with stone chimneys, etc., etc." from the unimproved hill farm they had moved to fifteen years earlier. But Tom had proved himself, had achieved a dream, and it was time to move on.

Talula later wrote: "I hated to move again and leave our nice home, as we had got everything around the place so convenient . . . but it seems it was the Lord's will for us to leave Cullman County. . . ."[1]

The move to the Limestone County farm was in some ways the most difficult move of all for Talula. It had become clear to everyone she could no longer manage without hired help, and it must have long before occurred to her the similarity of her daughter Almira's circumstances to her own at that age. Almira was twenty, had been doing woman's work for five or six years, and she still made most of the family's clothes. Since age seventeen, for seven months a year, Almira had put her side-saddle on the horse to ride the two miles in all kinds of weather to teach all ages of children in a little country school or at Logan. With some of the big country boys twice her size, rebellious, and dead set against learning anything, some days she despaired even of her own safety. Beautiful and refined, with several eager suitors, she would no doubt soon marry and leave home. Already her restlessness had resulted in her keeping company against her parents' wishes with a man who, in their opinion, was "not worthy of a woman of the highest standard of feminine virtue." He had an automobile and was well-established in business, "but her Papa would ten times rather see her dead and buried than to marry [that] rough fellow."[2]

One of the factors supporting Tom and Talula's earlier decision to move to Cullman County from Georgia had been its promotion as a place settled by "white folks,"[3] but the move had deprived Talula of the good, familiar help of the blacks as well as that of relatives in Fayette County. With Talula's illness, Almira, their auburn-haired daughter, had borne many of the burdens. Now the beautiful and talented young woman longed for a good education and a finer life. Limestone County offered better educational opportunities *and* the dependable help of black women for Talula.

The uncertainty of the years on Sand Mountain had prompted Talula, with Tom's approval, to keep title to the old Bottoms farm in Georgia. In addition, her father's death in 1906 had given her land that was entailed and could not be sold out of the family. Although Tom's aging brother George and his sons were managing the rental, those properties provided more trouble than income. Undoubtedly it was the crisis of Talula's alarming decline in health that prompted the urgent sale of most of her Georgia property in early 1913.[4]

It had been a good crop year, and harvest would not be complete until December, so the move could not be made until

New Bottoms home, *left,* on the Limestone County farm, built by Tom and his sons in 1914–15 from plans drawn up by George, provided space and a special place for Talula's quilting frame for the first time. It had four fireplaces and a cast-iron woodstove in the kitchen but no central heating, no electricity until 1937, and no indoor plumbing until 1940. Unpainted cottage, *right,* on the farm in Limestone County, Alabama, where Tom and Talula moved in winter of 1913–14, and where their daughter Almira was married to a prosperous thirty-five-year-old bachelor she had met just six weeks earlier.

then. Tom's grown sons would take the horse and buggy, the mules and wagons, and drive the cows sixty miles over dirt roads, transporting produce, dried and canned, for the family's winter food supply, seed for spring planting, farm implements, and household goods to their new location in Limestone County. Tom, Talula and Mollie Ruth would follow by train, for Talula's health was still too delicate to risk the long, jolting buggy ride to their new home.

A big auction was held and some things were disposed of beforehand. Talula even made the first effort (of two in her lifetime) to sell some of her quilts. A letter from a Montana woman who had been a fellow-patient at the sanitarium gives evidence that Talula made many more quilts during the Cullman years than the family needed: "I am sorry I cannot offer you something more flattering in regard to selling your quilts," Mrs. Hand wrote. "The Indians here are money poor . . . they make quilts of old pants and tobacco bags . . . and buy quilts . . . machine quilted . . . at the store. They sell for $3.00 or less a piece."[5]

The gap from October 1913 to June 1914 in what had been Talula's consistent habit of saving letters, no doubt resulted from the turmoil of moving from a nine-room dwelling to a small unpainted, cellarless cottage set on flat stones with only one small outbuilding. Five children ages ten to nineteen were still at home. Almira remained in Cullman County working for her room and board at Uncle Mattie's and teaching seven months of the year at a country schoolhouse near Logan. She was at home the rest of the time sewing for the family, picking or hoeing cotton, washing, and ironing to relieve her mother. It is not surprising she felt displaced and frustrated to the point of again thinking of marriage to the man of substantial means her parents felt sure she had left behind. When Talula found out Almira was still seeing the man, she determined to intervene. With the help of Almira's respected and much loved cousin Claude Bottoms, Talula succeeded in ending the liaison.[6]

By late 1915 the three sons still at home and their father had completed a new home on the Limestone County farm just in front of the house and nearer the road. They used seventeen-year-old George's plans. The boy was a brilliant student and the pride of his family. His design included large airy rooms with plastered walls, four fireplaces, and a big upstairs hall for Talula's quilting frame. The new clean house would end forever Talula's long "career" of scrubbing down bare plank walls and

We lived 15 years in Cullman County, and Papa came up here to see his brother and he liked this level part of the country. so began to make his arrangements to move here. I hated to have to move again and rather have staid there as we had got everything around the place so convenient, but Papa wanted to be in a more level country nearer town, so it would be more convenient And it seems it was the Lords will for us to leave Cullman County as everything here is more convenient and we are older and never could go ten miles to market now. This is lots better place for us old folks.

—Talula Bottoms, Memoir

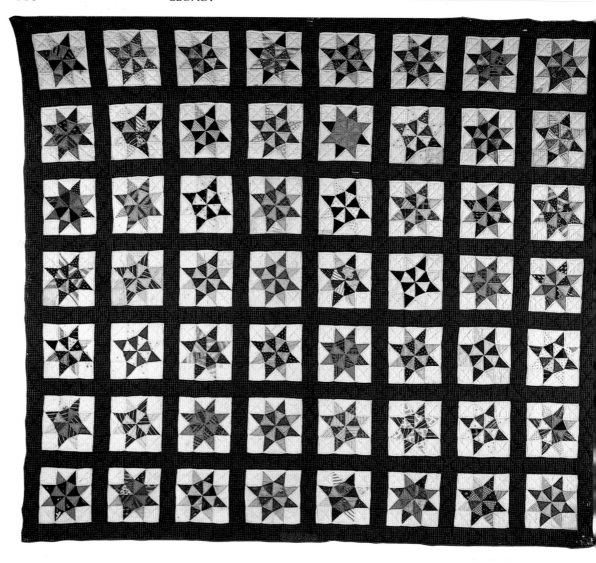

Eastern Star, c. late 1800s. One of the quilts given to Almira when she was married in 1915 and moved to Jackson County, Alabama, 50 miles away. Completely handmade of numerous scraps, the quilt was probably made from a pattern in use by nineteenth-century country women in Georgia. Susan Collins Bottoms's great-grandson still has an old quilt of this same design made by his great-grandmother.

Detail of *Eastern Star*.

floors with boiling water, and disinfecting baseboards in old houses to kill chinches and other insect pests. The new home was completed too late for Almira's marriage that year to the prosperous and respected bachelor farmer she had met through her brother Ary in May. Her marriage just six weeks later quite suddenly thrust her into a landed family with genteel manners, and she keenly felt her social limitations. It was a life that would make her "mistress" of a 3,000-acre "plantation," and enable her to leave behind forever the heavy, practical sewing, scrubbing, cotton picking—and the quiltmaking she so heartily disliked. Yet she took many of her mother's quilts with her including the *Eastern Star* which sixty-five years later would be passed on to her own daughter—to her farm home in Jackson County just fifty miles distant.

Talula's first letter saved after the move to Limestone County was written in June 1914, just three weeks before the outbreak of World War I. In it she apologized for her negligence in answering her children's letters ("but you don't know how busy we are and have been"), expressed regrets she could not attend graduation exercises for her son Matt in Battle Creek, and commented on one of the disadvantages of southern farm life: "We have flies, flies, flies, ten thousands, hundreds of millions and catch that many and that many more comes—but you know every 'sweet' must have its 'bitter.'" She went on to describe in detail the bountiful garden, sweet potato, and watermelon patches, tomato vines and "if we were at home in Cullman we would have ripe peaches, but someone else enjoys our labors now on that place."[7]

Nearly three years later World War I threatened the conscription of at least two sons, and it was a grave concern when the promising George was drafted. He had a deformed foot and felt he would soon be discharged, but his fine horsemanship placed him in training with a cavalry platoon at Camp Wheeler, Georgia, where he was assigned to help officers mount, to groom their horses, and to repair their bridles and saddles. He was close enough to visit Fayette County kinfolk and travelled there just before Christmas 1917. In an emotion-filled letter he reported to his parents of being overwhelmed by the love and attention of so many dear ones who still missed their favorite nephew and cousin after so many years.

In stunned disbelief his parents received a telegram informing them of their son's death January 20, 1918, an early casualty of a meningitis epidemic. The shock was compounded when his body was sent home in a casket too small for their stalwart son, and sealed, precluding the customary and healing ritual for the family of viewing the body at his funeral.[8]

It would be years before their anguish over the sudden death of this grown son would be relieved, for he was the first who had not experienced conversion to prepare him for life everlasting. If he had not been called into service, George would have graduated from the Agricultural School in Athens that year. Now his grieving family stood in silence and watched as the pallbearers, men of his senior class, lowered the olive drab casket into this first grave in a new family cemetery marked off in the very pasture where George had tended cows so recently. The women of his class each lifted a spade of earth and let it fall in sad farewell to their classmate and friend.

Several dozen letters were saved from that time of tribulation, and two of them were from Captain Edward C. Betts, George's commanding officer. They discuss a quilt that Talula

Sister Nannie Gilbert Dickson and her children. Left to Right: Oscar, William, Nannie, Johnnie May, Lela Maude and Lester Claude (twins). Nannie Gilbert was eleven when her mother died in 1865 at thirty-one. She was pregnant with Johnnie May when her husband Burke was killed under the wheels of his wagon-load of logs in 1891. After her second log home burned about 1900, Nannie moved into Fayetteville, though she still ran her farm and managed to send her four children to college. Most of her descendants still live in Fayette or Clayton counties.

had sent to her son at the army base. George was covered with that quilt when he was taken by ambulance to an Atlanta hospital; it was left there to be sterilized after his death and thought lost, but was later found and sent home to his mother.

At the time of George's death, Talula had three married children and seven grandchildren. "And when they began to get married, I felt very heartsick . . . because our family circle was broken . . . tho I soon got over it. . . ." But Talula's wider circle was to be broken again in a heart-rending way back home in Georgia. In 1924 her troubled sister, Nannie, took her own life at her home in Fayetteville. Talula made the sorrowful pilgrimage to be with her family and her sister's children for what she felt was the saddest funeral of her life.

Nannie had been unusually disturbed after George's death in 1918, and it had been as much for her sister's sake as for her own that Talula had made the sad but healing week-long visit to Fayette County in July of that year to talk out every detail of George's last contact with loved ones. At that time Nannie carried within her heart the dead weight of husband, two sons, and now this nephew; all seemed lost so tragically, and she could not let go of her grief. Her mother's death, too, still haunted her; and after John Gilbert's death in 1906, Nannie had been the one to plead most fervently with Talula and Tom to come back to Georgia to live.

This *Star* (unnamed), c. 1915–25, may have been a variation of Talula's *Glittering Star*, reflecting her ability to buy fabric during more prosperous times. She made at least two of these and may have made one for each of her children.

Lone Star quilt made especially for Almira in 1928 in colors she chose for one of the six bedrooms in her farm home in Jackson County, Alabama. Almira and Robert Butler by this time had seven children and their home was being expanded, decorated and furnished appropriately. Talula had previously made Mollie Ruth a *Lone Star* in her chosen colors: lavender, green, pink, blue, and yellow. Both quilts were cherished and have been perfectly preserved.

Pear Basket, left, c. 1880s. One of the "five or six nice pretty quilts" Talula made "before any children came to our home," and quilted in the 1890s. Given to her son Matt (David Mattison) after his marriage to Alice Kolvoord in December 1913, Matt's oldest daughter inherited it and passed it on to her only son in Texas. Much used and washed many times, this one-hundred-year-old quilt was successfully washed again just before this photograph was made, a tribute to its fine materials and workmanship. The homespun backing, probably woven by Elisa before her death in 1891, is sewn by hand from six thirty-inch squares and three eighteen-inch pieces suggesting Talula used those materials of necessity during the severe depression of the 1890s. Narrow, red, straight-cut binding expertly sewn by hand to the back has been turned over the front and stitched down by machine with black thread, no doubt soon after the purchase of Talula's first treadle machine in 1895. *Below:* Detail of *Pear Basket.*

In August 1905, almost a year before John Gilbert died, Nannie had written Talula a poignant letter—full of nostalgia for her mother and the good life she had known before the War. It was a telling reminder of the inordinate suffering of women whose lives of relative ease and security had been destroyed by the War and its aftermath. Nannie told of seeing once more "our cousin Puss Magnum," daughter of Holly Gilbert's half sister Sarah, and "the nearest living kin of women on our mother's side," who had left Georgia for Texas and a new life after her Aunt Holly's death. Cousin Puss had returned to Jonesboro forty years later and "wanted to see all of Ma's children. She told me more about our Mother's people than I ever knew—our great-grandmother was a Harrison, own cousin of President Harrison. . . ." Talula was puzzled when she tried to understand her sister's clinging to those lost dreams of genteel ancestry, when doing so brought sadness. But Nannie was her own "nearest kin of women," and that letter had been treasured for what it revealed of her dear sister's heart. When Talula got home from Georgia after her sister's funeral, she took it out with the rest of Nannie's letters, read them all, and gave herself up to weeping. As the days wore on, however, she felt a turbulence in her own heart she could not seem to shake.

For a year or longer before her sister's death Talula had received reports from Georgia relatives about Nannie's alarming decline, how she "talked off," lost touch with reality, and had waking nightmares of starvation, freezing, and burning harking back to the War years. Nannie had written Talula sporadically about her loneliness and despair. After Nannie's suicide attempt, a year earlier, Talula had wanted desperately to help her by having her come to Alabama to live, but it had been their son Matt's wise counsel that such an arrangement, though compassionate, would not help Nannie and might even exaggerate her symptoms, thus becoming a nightmare for Talula. Notwithstanding, Talula's grief was compounded by doubts after this tragic end to her sister's life. Instead of an obituary, she had only a sensational news story recounting every shocking detail of Nannie's death to put away with her sister's letters.

Talula had barely begun to pick up her own life when her gifted son Matt, mainstay of his parents and articulate counselor to his younger siblings, died suddenly and tragically in Battle Creek, leaving a wife and three young children. This new loss was possibly the greatest trial of her life, for Matt had become the interpreter of a fast-moving world to his old-fash-

T. J. Bottoms family and in-laws gathered in 1918 for the funeral of George who died of meningitis in an Atlanta hospital in January, an early victim of an epidemic that swept Camp Wheeler, Georgia, during World War I.

ioned parents and a mouthpiece for his father, who found it increasingly difficult to articulate the strong values of his old world to his children. Talula could not rise quickly from the shock, and Tom was bowed down with a grief so heavy it alarmed Talula. The distance and expense precluded travel to his funeral, and this time both parents were denied the healing grief in the ritual of mourning at the open casket of their son.

But Talula had to hold up, for Mollie Ruth was devastated by the great empty silence left by her brother's death. In 1914, soon after the move to Limestone County, Mollie Ruth had been close to death from typhoid fever when Matt left his medical work and returned home to nurse her back to health.

If Talula and Mollie Ruth were heavy laden by Matt's death, Tom seemed broken completely. His bowed shoulders as he took the milk bucket and walked slowly to the barn, his whiskery beard wet with tears, his quiet sobbing when he sat in his old Morris chair to read his Bible, wrung the hearts of his wife and daughter. They had to let go of their grief to comfort and encourage him. Talula reminded him of his brave mother Elisa who, after her son Bobbie's death in September 1890, had worked out her grief by spinning wool and knitting enough socks to buy three handsome mustache cups for her remaining sons. How proud she had been to get the socks finished in time to give the cups to Tom, Mattie, and George for Christmas.

Talula with brother, sisters, and in-laws, 1918. Before Talula's son George's death in January, he had spent a weekend in Fayette and Clayton counties visiting family. This picture was taken in July when Talula visited her family and talked out her grief with those last in contact with her son. Left to right: (standing) sister Bettie Stell, Walter Stell, sister-in-law Etta Gilbert and brother John James Calvin (Bud) Gilbert; (seated) Talula and sister Nannie Gilbert Dickson.

Talula began to piece a quilt especially for Tom; and Mollie Ruth, who soon had to return to Florence State Normal to finish her term, wrote "Papa" encouraging letters. In one she sent him a poem she had composed in memory of her "five dear brothers."

After mother and daughter had worked through this dark time together, they became like sisters who began to see Tom as something of a tragic hero they needed to heal. Before long, Tom responded, becoming aware of farm sounds: birds' songs, the calls of "gee" and "haw," the clanging of iron on stone as mules pulled the plows for sons tilling the soil for spring sowing. When he began to get out of bed, pull on his pants, and hook his suspenders at 4:30 in the morning again, and Talula heard him shaking down the ashes to build her breakfast fire in the stove, she knew he would survive.

Once again Tom and Talula Bottoms arose from the trials and overwhelming losses of those early Limestone County years to enter a time of liberation impossible in their earlier life together. Tom with his cotton farming, Talula with her fine flocks, gardening, and quiltmaking were beginning the years of their greatest personal achievement and productivity.

CHAPTER 16

Triumph and Letting Go

T om felt a modest pride in at last making a good living after getting established on the farm in Limestone County. He felt sure he would be able to leave his children the legacy he had long dreamed of, a piece of land for each.

Long an inventor of improved farm machinery, he began to try once more, though with little success, to get patents and market some of his ideas. His experiments with developing a long-grained, boll-weevil resistant cotton were finally successful, and by the late twenties he was getting more orders for his Bottoms cotton seed than he could fill. Three sons were now local farmers raising his cotton, and some were winning prizes on it. They had been given a start by their father's gift of land.[1]

For the first time Talula could indulge her love of yard and garden flowers in addition to the potted plants overflowing her big veranda. She continued to grow and improve her flocks of prize chickens and ducks, and occasionally she was able to buy whole bolts of calico to make whatever kinds of quilts she wanted. Tommie's cotton was perfectly suited to easy carding, and with fewer burdens and good help when she needed it, Talula felt fortunate indeed. Many of her children and grandchildren were in and out, as well as a never-ending stream of company—relatives from Cullman County and Georgia, Tennessee, and Texas, and neighbors and friends from nearby. Although she was never completely well, she felt stronger than she had for twenty years and rarely did anything slow her down. She and Tom continued to get up at 4:30 in the morning, a lifetime ritual, build a fire in the old cast-iron stove, and finish

Tom Bottoms, *right,* (about 1925) picking the long-grained, boll-weevil-resistant cotton he developed on the Limestone County, Alabama, farm and sold widely during the 1920s. Tom carefully picked and sorted cotton from the earliest and finest bolls, and he and his children hand-seeded that cotton over a number of years to perfect the "Bottoms Cotton." *Far right:* Talula with grandchildren Nancilu and Jim Ed (seated) and Ruth, oldest children of Almira Butler, at Glendale Farm, Woodville, Alabama, 1920. Almira had just given birth to her fourth child, and Talula was there to help. Although it was July and very warm, Talula wore a long-sleeved dress. She always felt it would be immodest to show her arms in public and rarely rolled up her sleeves even at home except to plunge her hands into the hot tubs of water outdoors and use her "rubboard" to do the family wash.

their breakfast and kitchen work by 5:30. Because of such habits, Talula had long and productive days to work on quilts. As they began to fill up the old trunk, her face seemed to grow younger and her step lighter; the flowers in the big yard bloomed profusely in response to her careful and happy cultivation.

But the hard times that fell on the nation in 1929 and the Great Depression following struck this family also. One son lost his cotton farm and the land his father had given him. He also lost land given to a younger brother who had co-signed with him, and the old parents were in danger of losing their home. Talula wrote to her daughter that they were considering sale of their farm because "if we miss one payment the land bank will take it." The needs of their children had always come first. Perhaps they took too much responsibility for them, for they had sold 119 acres of land in 1920 and had later mortgaged their home to help two of their children get more education than their parents could ever imagine; they had lifted other children out of financial difficulty resulting from the Crash of 1929. Both Tom and Talula made efforts to persuade some of their children to invest in farms nearby as prices fell and land was cheap, for to them land meant survival, no matter how hard the times. They worried about their children's debts. Talula began having "curious spells" diagnosed as angina, and

Dutch Doll I, *left,* c. 1930s. Talula began to make her series of "little girl" quilts in the late twenties when a young granddaughter, her namesake, saw a picture of one and asked "Grandma" to make her one. (That granddaughter now lives in California and no picture of her quilt, which she still has, is available. It is thought to be made in the design shown above.) Talula then set about making little girl quilts for each of her fifteen granddaughters. Eleven are known to exist today, some much worn though still treasured. A quilt of similar design, *Sunbonnet Girls*—dated "first quarter of 20th century"—is pictured in *Quilts in America* by Patsy and Myron Orlafsky, McGraw Hill.) *Above:* Detail of *Dutch Doll I.*

Tommie began to feel like an old man. Like a ritual of return to the source of life, however, Talula's letters to loved ones and their replies from kin in Georgia renewed and sustained her. The hard times seemed to stimulate rather than discourage her quiltmaking.

In the late twenties one of her granddaughters, a namesake, saw a picture or pattern for a *Sunbonnet Girl* quilt in one of the many pattern books, flyers, and farm magazines Talula received. She asked if her grandmother could make her a quilt like that. Talula had thirteen granddaughters and knew if she made a quilt for this one, she would want to make one for all. She had recently made a *Lone Star* quilt for Mollie Ruth, was working on another for Almira, and probably had other quilts in process as well. Nevertheless, she soon made the quilt for Lula, one of several granddaughters named for her, and another for her sister Sarah, for their family was about to move to a distant state. Once she started on a project, her energy increased and she became as lighthearted and eager as a child.

The challenge Talula had set for herself in making these quilts grew and took on increasing variety. Two more grand-daughters were born in 1929 and 1931. The *Sunbonnet Girls* quilts grew to forty-eight blocks and departed from the original colors and arrangement, adding a third inner border. One un-usual quilt has fifty-four proud little bosomy girls walking in six vertical rows up and down the quilt with plum-colored plain sashing between. In this quilt the girls were stuffed with cotton as they were appliquéd to give them a three-dimensional look.

Talula's completion of this group of quilts (representing her devotion to her granddaughters) is symbolic of the depth of her love for all her children and their families. Her true legacy was the example she set in the life she lived. But her quilts were the tangible evidence, her love made manifest. Although she car-ried until the end of her life certain habits and attitudes toward her family characteristic of the "sentimentalism of the seven-ties," as Ruth Finley calls it,[2] her love was no sentimental mat-ter. The diminutives of *Tommie*, *Burlie*, and *Mollie* stuck with her husband and children; she called all of her twenty-five grandchildren "Honey Dear" (in part because there were so many names to remember). She found it difficult to let go of her children and allow them to follow their dreams; but her love was expressed in everything she did, so they knew it had a solid foundation. In time they would have her quilts to prove it.

Talula and Tom Bottoms revealed by their lives an unusual energy grounded in their close connection with the land. They were practical people who created their own lives out of what it produced, but they were also sustained by a strong and simple faith in another world to come. Those two worlds for them were never truly separate and distinct. God walked the fields and woods with Tom, and Talula felt His presence in all of nature and in her hands as she worked. Both knew they were created to be *doers* with whatever was at hand. They kept written records, wrote letters, made things; they built their own houses; and like the Amish today, they helped their neighbors build and rebuild when there was a need. Wherever they lived, they knew their neighbors well and cared about them, shared their sorrows and joys and their homes with them; and well into the twentieth century Talula and her daughters made almost every-thing they needed to cover themselves, their families, and their beds. It was as if they had never left behind the old world of craftsmanship and mutual dependence. Except for the times when she was wholly disabled, Talula never stopped piecing quilts.

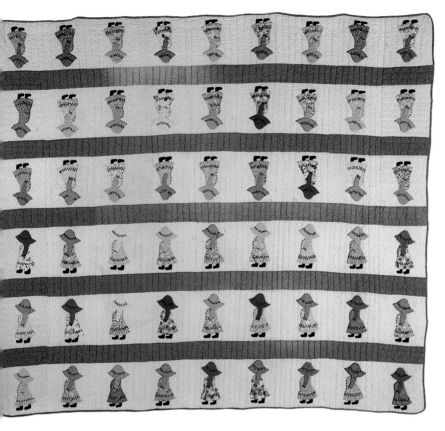

Dutch Doll II, c. 1930s. Like many of Talula's quilts, this one is well-travelled, from Alabama to Michigan, to California and back to Michigan. Talula's pleasure in seeing her granddaughters' delight in having their very own quilts, and her habit of never making two alike, resulted in this unique arrangement of dolls. The little girls look more like proud little women; their bodies were stuffed as they were appliquéd on to give them a three-dimensional look.

Sunbonnet Sue, left, c. 1930s. This popular pattern was made in dainty colors for one granddaughter, but the quilt remained tucked away in a cedar chest from 1946 until Almira's death in 1980 when it was passed on to one of Talula's great-great-granddaughters. *Above:* Detail of *Sunbonnet Sue.*

Colonial Girl, c. 1930s. Talula used a pattern she ordered from *The Country Gentleman* to make this and several other little-girl quilts. She saved the clipping from an Edna Gugenheim column, "Nancy's Patchwork Bedroom," which calls it *Oldfashioned Sunbonnet Girl* and offers the pattern to anyone for a three-cent stamp. This was one of Talula's last little-girl quilts, made for her youngest granddaughter.

"Before the Centennial decade [1880s] was over, there would be a new world . . . In the new world there would be no need for women to bend patient eyes and fingers over patchwork," Ruth Finley wrote in 1929.[3] The Industrial Revolution of the nineteenth century Finley speaks of was accelerated a thousand fold by the twentieth-century computerized world of technology. Its impersonal machinery would remove the need for people to create with their own hands the things they used in everyday life. Yet with each current month's periodicals, more and more events prove the re-emergence of creative expression in arts and craftwork of all kinds, suggesting, as John Naisbitt has observed, that craftsmanship in our time fulfills a basic need and is an antidote to high-tech culture.[4]

Another profound change from old world to new that occurred in the last quarter of the nineteenth century resulted from the bomb-shell of Charles Darwin's theory of evolution. Any vestige of the shock waves that may have filtered into the rural communities of Georgia and Alabama served only to bind

Detail of *Colonial Girl.*

the people closer to their churches and their faith. "We had never read the Bible and studied it enough to know its teachings, and . . . loved to hear the preacher read and explain the scripture, and the good old time religion . . . they did not have [song] books but sang 'on a credit,' as they called it . . . and Oh! how it stirred to souls of the people."[5]

Tom had gone to school long enough to learn to read, and after he was ordained to preach he had begun to study the Bible for his own understanding. Tom's influence was so strong, two of his sons became Seventh Day Baptist ministers, and, in fact, most of his children and many of his grandchildren never departed from the basics of his faith. It must have been painful therefore for the parents for whom "belief in Christ was . . . a matter of life and death"[6] to see others of their children, with equal conviction, unable to experience the traditional "conversion" or the tenets of their father's beliefs.

Doubly painful to the aging parents as hard times fell on them in 1931 was the repeated reminder that their son George had died so young without public profession of his faith. Thirteen years after his death, the Veterans Administration was still questioning Tom and Talula's right to a "death compensation as dependent parents of George D. Bottoms XC-6, 084" due to the "non-production of primary evidence—a birth certificate or a church record of baptism".[7] No record of births was kept in Georgia in 1896 except in family Bibles, and perhaps this finally was the evidence that allowed them the "$16.50 per month for twenty years" that had been due them since 1918. According to their son Gilbert, the only one of their children still living today, they did eventually receive a small monthly check.

The spiritual source of Tom and Talula's simple "faith of their fathers" was continually renewed by letters from home reporting all religious happenings in Fayette County, with daily worship at home and the occasional meetings held by themselves or by visiting Seventh Day Baptist preachers at the family church Tom and his sons had organized. Both he and Talula felt secure in their faith and its interrelationship with farming the land. They drew their strength from both, and as some of their children made educational and scientific leaps into the twentieth century, it was more than they could comprehend. With their foundations so intricately bound to the folkways of simple farm people, Tom and Talula did not realize, nor did their children, how these two faithful people had hardly emerged from the old natural world with its strong mythologies and primitive practices. Neither did they understand then what a strong bridge the parents provided between that old world and the new for their children.

Mollie Ruth, for example, took her brother Matt's place as "interpreter" some years after his death. If she lacked his diplomacy, she compensated by kind and persistent probing to understand "what went on back then," before and after she was born in 1901. Even so she was shocked to learn, in talking with her older sister Almira, that she herself had been "cunjered."

> When you were a little baby, you got the thrash and it seemed that nothing Mamma could do for it would help. Women kept begging her to get old man Gurley to cunjer it away. They said that he could cunjer it and it would never come back any more. So one day he was there at the house— Mrs. Pierce and Miss Vinie and Mrs. Gurley were all there too, she decided to let him cunjer it. He said that he would have to take the baby down in the woods where nobody could see what he did or the cunjer wouldn't work. So he took you off down there in the woods and I imagine that he rubbed out your mouth with the crushed leaves of some sort of shrub; I imagine that he knew of a remedy that he knew nobody would believe in if they knew what it was. And you got well right straight. Mamma was convinced then that he had some kind of magic power.[8]

Mollie Ruth went on to earn honors in high school and college, became a college professor of English and writing, a published poet and essayist, a member of International Who's Who in Poetry, and a gifted teacher of poets. Perhaps the high point of her academic career was persuading Robert Frost to visit the Edmond campus of Oklahoma University (where she taught) for a lecture and seminar with her poetry classes in 1939.[9] It was Mollie Ruth who began to save her mother's letters, who encouraged Talula to write about the old times, who inspired some of her mother's finest 1930s quilts.

Mollie Ruth was the most intellectual member of her family and felt great responsibility for bridging the cultural and educational gaps dividing many of them. She was thorough in researching her novel (which was to be a major instrument of that bridge) and found her father a rich source of folklore:

> Everyone believed in scarifying. Pap was a scarifier and I done it after him. I guess the old scarifying horn is here somewhere now. Get it, Mamma.
>
> You just take this horn and put it on a baby's back and suck the blood to the surface. Then you take a sharp knife or a razor and cut right fine little gashes all over the red place and suck it again through the horn. Then it bleeds and you take the blood in a spoon and make the baby drink it. They claim that that will cure bold hives, or keep the baby from having them. Whether it helps the baby or not, there's nothing about it to hurt it, except what little pain it may feel, which can't be very much. The babies cry mightily when that's done to them. They cry all the time it's being done, but it don't hurt them much.
>
> Bold hives kill a baby mighty quick, and mothers will do anything they can think up to keep their children from taking them.[10]

At least one of the "scarified" babies was fifth son Roger, born in 1890. As a youth Roger puzzled and exasperated his parents; they despaired of his ever "making anything of himself," because he was a tinkerer and reader and did not like farm work. By seventeen, Roger had convinced them he *must* have an education; so he was sent to Alabama's Jacksonville Training School along with his nineteen-year old brother Ary, where he was placed in seventh grade and apologized to his parents for needing eighty-five cents a week for food. Within eight years Roger had been identified as a genius, was working ten hours a day for Maxwell Motor Co. (later Chrysler Corp.) in Detroit,

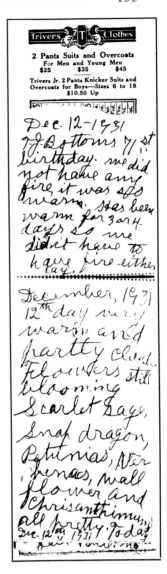

Pages from a weather journal Talula kept, December 1931.

going to the University of Michigan, and translating books on chemistry from the German language (which he had taught himself in his spare time).[11] His achievements during and after serving as a pilot and a trainer of officers in hydrogen production for the Navy in World War I are numerous; a final one was the development of an air purification system that enabled the *Nautilus* (the world's first Nuclear-powered submarine) to circle the globe under water. He had in fact "gone from the very bottom of the scale through to the top," with notable contributions to science and industry that are taken for granted today.[12]

The unbounded energy and inventiveness of their parents was, in fact, passed on to all Tom and Talula's children, though their unique and individual expressions of it created geographical and sometimes ideological distances beyond their parents' comprehension. One daughter and one son, however, remained close by until the end of their lives.

Almira, who lived just fifty miles away with her husband, Robert L. Butler, and their large family, was the busy mother of eight children and an "angel of mercy" to her parents and a dozen sharecropper families. Burlie had married Alice, his brother Matt's widow, and they came back finally to remodel the home and take care of Tom and Talula in their last years. But it possibly was the close connection and open communication with the younger daughter, Mollie Ruth, that contributed most to Talula's creative expression in writing and quiltmaking during her later years.

CHAPTER 17

The Quilter

Talula's niece Mollie died suddenly in 1928, and her letters ceased. Talula copied the obituary and then sent the clipping back to its author. Its opening words were, "And I heard a voice from heaven saying—*Write*, blessed are they which die in the Lord . . . that they may rest from their labors. . . ." The passionate tribute had been written by Mollie's brother Claude, Tom's talented nephew and their own daughter's singing teacher who Talula would always believe had saved Almira from a fate worse than death. How hard it must have been for Talula to lose this niece, more like a sister to her than her own sisters and a person to whom she could open her heart more completely even than she could to Tom! But Claude's words of assurance lifted her heart, and she put his copied words away with Mollie's letters that were, and still are, so full of life with all its ridiculous absurdities, its tragedies, its joys and triumphs. The appropriateness of those words must have occurred to Talula; they were from a passage Mollie herself had underscored in her own Bible.[1] She had doubly underscored *write*. Mollie had been the most faithful of all Talula's Georgia kinfolk. Their letters to each other had deepened their devotion, kept both vitally alive.

After Mollie's death, Talula turned to her daughter Mollie Ruth for sharing the details of daily life, and Mollie Ruth began consistently to save her mother's letters. Money was so scarce that at times the cheapest material "from Joe off the Truck" was all Talula could afford for making quilts, and Mollie Ruth began sending her cloth for quilting from Oklahoma City. She had become concerned about her mother's health and knew that quilt work did her a lot of good. When Mollie Ruth began to encourage her mother to write about her early life, it was in part because Mollie Ruth planned to write a novel based on her parents' lives. "Now Mamma," she wrote early in 1934, "you let

Mollie (Mary Elizabeth Bottoms, 1868–1928) and Jim Bottoms, children of Tom's brother George Washington Bottoms, in front of the old Fayette County log home built in 1866 and later covered with plank sheeting. Mollie devoted her young years to caring for her parents, and did not marry Tom Simpson until she was in her fifties and both sets of parents had died. Mollie made all her own clothes, as well as her father's and her brothers', cultivated beautiful flowers and wrote innumerable letters to her Aunt Lula's family in Alabama. Like her mother, Susan Collins Bottoms, and her Aunt Talula, she was a fine quilter, though most of her quilts have been worn out or lost. The four that remain are much worn: a *Flying Geese,* an *Irish Chain,* a *Double T's* and an *Eastern Star.*

everybody get their quilt pieces done the best way they can. I have something else I want you to do for awhile . . . Read this book and then write down things about your own family, and Papa's and neighbors and the nature of living conditions when you were a child . . . I am going to send you paper to write on. . . ."[2]

About the same time—unknown to Mollie Ruth—her oldest brother Ary had suggested the same thing to "Mamma and Papa," and sent them the little book that was saved for ten years before Talula wrote a line in it. Talula did, however, begin to make notes on the paper her daughter sent her, and over the years filled sixty-five pages with notes she entitled "My Life and Reminiscences from my Earliest Remembrance."

But news kept coming from Georgia that surviving relatives and friends of Talula's generation were feeble or sick or "very low and not expected to live," and Talula longed to make one more pilgrimage to the land of her childhood. By late summer she had persuaded her son Burlie and wife, Alice, to take her and her daughter Almira back to visit the places and people she knew and loved as a child. Talula's account of that journey was recorded in an eighteen-page letter to "My Dear Children and Grandchildren in the U.S.," which came back finally to be saved by its author in "Ary's little tool chest Papa gave him when he was 3 or 4 years old."[3] Inspiration and renewal are reflected in every detail of that letter as Talula reports the drama and comedy as vividly as she had done thirty-three years before of her more harrowing "excursion" trip to Georgia by train with five young children.

The *Dahlia* (or *Star Flower*), *above left*, c. 1930–40s. Talula tells of having seen "the old, old *Dahlia* quilt of my stepgrandmother's" in Fayetteville in 1934, and she may have begun this quilt by piecing some of the blocks after her visit to her childhood home. She carefully hand-pieced 70 twelve-inch stars of gay floral prints and checks on muslin background, but never sewed them into a quilt. Many years after her death, this quilt was made from 35 of those blocks by Talula's daughter-in-law Alice and quilted by her. Another *Dahlia* quilt was recently hand-made from the other 35 blocks, plus seven more she pieced herself, by a granddaughter in Florida who inherited through her mother Nettie (Talula's son Emmett's wife), much of Talula's unfinished work. (See Dorothy Frager, *The Book of Sampler Quilts*, p. 94, for a similar pattern.) *Above:* Detail of *Dahlia*.

Lifeboat II, c. 1936. Talula never ceased to feel that her daughters were a special gift to add joy to her life, and she never made a special quilt for one without making one of the same design for the other. This one was made for Almira for her "blue bedroom." The unusual combination of peach, blue, red, and white was chosen by Talula, and the quilt remains today in that same bedroom, now used as a guest room by Almira's son and daughter-in-law. (See *Uncoverings 1984*.)

The *Lifeboat, above,* c. 1935, was Talula's name for this very old pattern (its origin lost in time) traditionally called *Whig's Defeat.* The pattern was named for the Whig party probably before the presidential election of 1852, when the party went out of existence (See Safford and Bishop's *American Quilts and Coverlets,* p. 121). An earlier Arkansas version called the *Democrat* (c. 1826) is discussed in Michael Luster's *Stitches in Time* (pages 5 and 6), and another called *True Lover's Knot* (c. 1800?) was reputed to be the "most beautiful quilt on the back of Lookout Mountain" when it was seen in 1971. (Bets Ramsey in "Design Invention in Country Quilts,"

(Continued on page 141.)

During her visit Talula had asked to see two old quilts from her mother's and her grandmother's generations:

October 22, 1934 . . .

At Johnnie May's we saw the old, old "Dahlia" quilt of my step grandmother's. . . .

Then we went to my brother Bud's across the street and I spent that night with him, for I had not seen him. He was the one that came so near dying in the summer . . . Well, while at Bud's I got to talking about the old quilt of my mother's that went to Bud. So Etta got it to show to me, and I asked her to let me bring it home with me to try to get the pattern and make a square. So she did and I have made one square. It is very, very pretty, and as none of us knew the name of it I have named it "The Life Boat," as the 5 blue corner pieces resemble oars more than anything. The center can be the boat and have 5 oars at each of the four corners. It is made in red, white, and blue.[4]

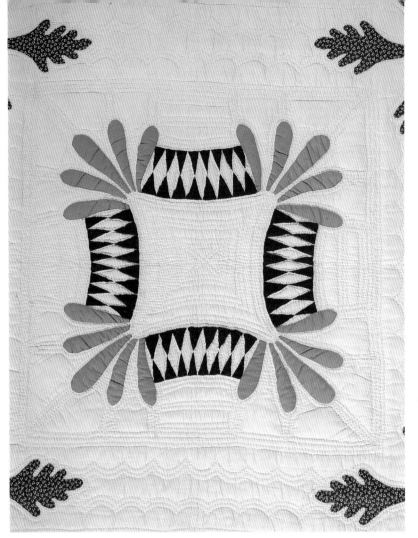

Uncoverings 1980). In Talula's quilt the five blue "oars" at the corners of each square are pieced to four little tornado shaped funnels of fine white fabric, while tiny red triangles are sewn to little diamonds of white to form the four sides of the "boats." The 145 pieces in each of the nine squares are completely hand-pieced; only the oak-leaf crosses at intersection points are appliquéd. Talula has relieved the severity of the red, white, and blue pattern by choosing a red calico print with tiny yellow flowers for the crosses and for the old-fashioned narrow binding. The quilt's significance for Talula is underscored by her having saved the brown paper patterns hand drafted from her mother's quilt as well as a trial square she made first of cheaper material. (This quilt was first pictured and discussed in *Uncoverings* 1984). Above: Detail of *Lifeboat.*

The spontaniety and enthusiasm of this letter is reflected in an extraordinary number of letters Talula wrote Mollie Ruth during the next ten years; so many of them mention quilts it is apparent Mollie Ruth had begun to look upon her mother's quiltmaking as something quite remarkable. Mother and daughter reported every detail of everyday life to each other, encouraging and advising each other; and Talula's progress on the *Lifeboat,* once she had started the pieced quilt, was regularly reported, for she was making it for Mollie Ruth.

The significance of that quilt in Talula's large body of work can be better understood when it is compared with others she made in the 1930s. She deliberately challenged herself to make this one comparable to the "nice pretty quilts" she had made in the 1880s soon after her marriage and quilted in the 1890s. It was in fact made just fifty years after *The Feather,* one of her own most treasured quilts which was also to go to Mollie Ruth. Was it because the *Lifeboat* was more difficult to make than the

Princess Feather, top, 1936–38. A picture of an appliquéd quilt like this was sent to Talula from Michigan in mid-1930s by her granddaughter Mary Bottoms. About a year later, Talula presented the finished quilt to Mary as a surprise. It was probably made by Pattern No. 300, Talula's 1928 catalog, Ladies Art Company, St. Louis, MO, Quilt Patterns: Patchwork and Appliqué. (Courtesy of Mary Bottoms Wentworth, Ridge Top, Tennessee.) *Bottom:* Detail of *Princess Feather*.

other quilts like those of her mother's generation that she had not tried it before?

Letters saved from 1935 report family and community events, the weather, health and sickness, fires and accidents, work in the garden, a new calf born, much talk about listing houses for sale or losing them to the land bank, and flowers so beautiful people slow down to look as they pass the house; "I still hoe my own flowers, but I feel better when I do." When political rhetoric promised old people $200 a month in the proposed Townsend Plan, Talula wrote, "Well, we are not expecting the $200 a month, but I have already planned to spend it as fast as we get it, as that is the way it must be done. . . . You just ought to see what all I am going to have done to this house and yard, etc., etc. Tho you won't be apt to see any such thing."[5]

Though Talula's habit by this time was to have several quilts in progress; her letters from that summer mention only the *Colonial Girl* she made for Mollie Ruth. She was still working on the difficult *Lifeboat* blocks, for by October she had that quilt in her frame, and wrote her daughter:

> I have to be very busy these days to get as much done on my quilt as I can before cold weather comes. I cannot go up to quilt when it is very cold; if I go up now will have to wrap up good. Have been wrapping the old overcoat around my feet and around my lap, tho will have more wrapping if I go up tomorrow I think. . . ."[6]

Talula's quilting frame was set up in the big upstairs hall—twelve feet wide—which her son George, who designed the house, had in mind for the frame. The hall was hot in summer and cold in winter, for the only heat in the house was from the downstairs fireplaces and the kitchen stove. Her son Gilbert remembers she almost always had a quilt in her frame. Other letters indicated sheer joy and intense excitement as Talula worked daily except on the Sabbath and Sunday. Those days she rested her tired hands and sore fingers until Monday so she could "go it again as fast as I can."[7] She quilted the *Lifeboat* in about six weeks and used more than six hundred yards of thread, a lot of quilting indeed when the relatively small size of the quilt is considered (72″ x 84″). A few old bloodstains on the backing are reminders that pricked fingers and tired hands were no deterrent to achieving her goal. Her completion of this quilt was a major triumph, and her chosen name for it undoubtedly significant, though perhaps unconsciously so. As an example of her best work and a symbol of the creative passion of her own

Pink Piney, above, c. 1930s, was quilted by Beulah Clark (now Webb) who charged Almira eight dollars seven years after Talula's death when Almira inherited "25 or 30" quilt tops in 1946. The name of this quilt came from *Yesterday's Quilts in Homes of Today.* An old "Piney" (peony) quilt then owned by Carlie Sexton is pictured on page nine of that booklet. (Ordered from *Successful Farming,* Meredith Publishing Company, Des Moines, Iowa, in 1930, the booklet was found among Talula's quilt patterns.) Talula also made an unusual lavender *Piney* quilt that has never been quilted, and gave it to her foster son's wife. Carl and Myrle had four daughters and Talula made a quilt for each of them. *Left:* Detail of *Pink Piney.*

Garden Bouquet, above. Talula pieced and appliquéd this quilt for her daughter Mollie Ruth, probably in 1932, and may have quilted it soon after. It is the first of at least five quilts Talula made by this Nancy Page design in the 1930s, the series of patterns and instructions clipped from Florence LaGanke's column in the *Nashville Banner* February–July, 1932. It is documented by the saved clippings and the much-perforated, tissue paper patterns Talula used to cut out the pieces. (A similar quilt is shown in photograph of a Clemmie Pugh and her quilts in *A People and Their Quilts* by John Rice Irwin.) The series of patterns and Florence LaGanke's instructions have recently been republished. (See *Country Needlecraft,* February, 1987, and subsequent issues.) *Top right:* Detail of *Garden Bouquet.*

life, it marked the apex of her "career," lifted her above a sea of troubles, and introduced what was to be her most productive period of quiltmaking. For the rest of the thirties and into the forties, with few exceptions, when she found an unusually pretty pattern she did not make just one quilt or two; she set about to make seven quilts like it, one for each of her children. Certainly her journey back to her childhood home in 1934 was like a pilgrimage to the Castalian Spring,[8] for what followed was a veritable explosion of expression in both writing and quiltmaking.

There is the beautiful *Dahlia,* perhaps like the quilt of her step-grandmother's, made with a gathered flower in the center of each star block,[9] and the *Princess Feather* in red and white with a pale blue border made and quilted as a surprise in 1937 or 1938 for a granddaughter who sent her a picture of one from Michigan; the *Pink Piney* and *Purple Piney,* several *Double Wedding Rings* and *Fancy Dresden Plates,* all patterns popular in the thirties. One quilt design that shows her love for "laid work," as she called appliqué, was the *Garden Bouquet* made with twenty different appliquéd flowers "growing" in little pieced urns with a "meek bird and a saucy bird" perched on each one. Its interesting variety and Greek Key border so appealed to her that she made at least five, and worked away at her happy task with such eagerness and joy she became herself like a little smooth-running, precision machine. During that time she began to order bags of scraps from Sears Roebuck, or from ads that appeared in farm magazines, and she mixed some of them with scraps from her daughter's sewing to make a dozen or more *Sunflowers* and many *Grecian Stars.* The speed with which she could piece these quilts with their odd shapes and curved patches was astonishing.

Finally there were the *Grandmother's Fans* and *Improved Nine Patches* that kept her hands busy until the very end of her life. All the while her letters kept Mollie Ruth closely in touch.

Bluebirds in Easy Appliqué, c. 1936. Talula's perforated patterns cut from brown paper, and a clipping from the *Nashville Banner,* February 18, 1936, name this quilt. A depression quilt, this is a tied "comfort," the squares pieced from old clothes given Talula by her daughter Almira, and filled with hand-carded wool from Glendale Farm sheep. All the fabrics in this quilt have a depression story to tell. It was made for granddaughter Ruth Butler when she was ill with tuberculosis, and the charming birds were appliquéd on to cheer her. Ruth treasures this quilt above all of her many heirlooms because she credits it, and all it represented of her grandmother's love, with saving her life. She thinks the birds in black were symbols of the gloomy prospects for her recovery.

Before their son Matt died, he had asked his parents to take a young orphan boy from Battle Creek to raise. Matt had nursed the child's dying grandfather and had promised he would find a good home for the boy. Carl Leake became Tom and Talula's youngest son; Talula made quilts for his family as well as her own children's families. Her quilts became more widely known as her children migrated to distant states; some won prizes at county and state fairs as far away as Ohio and New York. Talula chose not to compete but simply to follow her own dreams and visions. Making quilts was the emotional center of her life, the natural flowering of her creative capacities, and she gave no more thought to competition with others in her craft than one of her rose bushes would think to compete with a dahlia. As Lucille Hilty has so movingly expressed, "making a quilt is an organic process, closely related to the deepest feelings one has about life and the society in which one lives . . . It is the union of the hands with the mind and the spirit. . . ."[10] For Talula, whose identity seemed never to have been threatened by changing styles and popular trends, her quilt work was as central to her physical and emotional health as her rural environment and the country air she breathed. She could not waste her precious energy on competition either in fashion or with other quiltmakers.

Her way of responding to any of her family's troubles or illnesses was to do what she could to help and to make tangible her love in the gift of a quilt. How quickly she could make such a gift if an appropriate one was not readily available from her trunk! An example:

> Fayetteville, GA
> Feb. 14, 1941

"Dearest Aunt Lula:
. . . You can't imagine how much I did enjoy Uncle Will being with us during his recent illness . . . he was the first to use your beautiful quilt, & he was so proud to do so . . . you must have thought I could use it for sickness . . . is why you made such a long heavy one, it tucks in so good on my bed. [11]

In the winter of 1935–36 Talula learned a granddaughter was growing thin and weak, threatened with tuberculosis. Talula was all too familiar with the dread disease, because her mother, her stepmother, two brothers and a sister had died of it. Her response in this case was to make a *Bluebirds in Easy Appliqué* quilt for the granddaughter, a warm one because of "TB's" characteristic chills and fever. [12] No quilt she created is more expressive of her ingenuity, for the quilt makes a statement so moving it belies the bag of old clothes that was its material source. Though Talula's is a depression quilt made mostly from good parts of worn out wool clothes, some of which had already served two or more family members as hand-me-downs or "made-overs," it speaks eloquently of her love. The quilt has many stories to tell, for the old clothes represent very hard times for her daughter Almira's large family when it was touch-and-go whether they would lose their farm and the home inherited by her husband from his father. Talula's magic does wonders with those cast-offs; she made crazy patch blocks and then appliquéd on alternate plain blocks in new wool of many colors a pair of little birds looking trustfully upward.

The quilt reflects Talula's lifetime of giving all to others in creative ways, her love and compassion, as well as her genius in "making something from nothing." Her granddaughter got well; she and that quilt for many years were inseparable, and she later used it to cover her own children when they were sick or when they simply needed something warm and soft and made by loving hands to give them a feeling of comfort and security.

CHAPTER 18

Fulfillment

Tom Bottoms resisted mightily when his children wanted to give him a battery-operated radio for Christmas in 1937. They saw how happily occupied Talula was with her quiltmaking and how troubled their aging father was about the alarming state of the world with all its sin and violence and the growing threat of war in Europe. In spring of that year he had been felled by what appeared to be a "stroke";[1] and though he amazed the doctors with his recovery, his eyes were getting dim and he could no longer without great effort and discouragement write his convictions of the truth, his admonitions to Editors of the *Nashville Banner*, the *Atlanta Constitution*, and the *Birmingham News* as he had done for so many years. "A radio was the very last thing I ever wanted!" he stormed in his powerful voice that sometimes frightened his grandchildren. But within weeks he was listening to the early morning gospel programs and to every newscast of the day. His face and eyes took on a new energy and life, and the timbre of his voice could be heard again, not complaining but expressing the thoughts of his still active mind and his emotional responses to what he heard, for he cared deeply about the world and its people.

So accustomed were these two old people to their modest comforts, they had hardly missed what all their children by the mid-thirties took for granted as necessities. Oil lamps were their indoor lighting, fireplaces or the cast-iron stove their heat, and the old well with its bucket and chain so convenient just outside the kitchen door was their sole water supply. The well served also as a refrigerator in summer for butter and milk, let down by rope into the same dark cold from which the water was drawn up for drinking, cooking, bathing, scrubbing, and washing. The black pot for heating water and boiling clothes still stood by the washtubs in the back yard, and down past the chicken house and the woods was the house of convenience with its handy Sears catalog, where Tom continued to "take his walks" summer and winter as long as he lived.

It wasn't until the late thirties that they agreed to let their son Burlie put in electricity and afterward were glad to accept a refrigerator from their son Roger. (It would be several more years before they would have water piped into the house.) Talula was proud of that wonderful refrigerator that saved her so many steps and the handling of the long buckets full of milk in summer up and down inside the well. She would never forget how she had provoked Tommie's quick temper one summer by spilling a whole bucket of milk into the well. For a month or longer they had to haul water from cousin George Walker's well across the road, and not a day passed during that time of inconvenience that Tommie did not raise his voice in protest of her carelessness.[2]

Then, after the frightening experiences of Tom's illness in 1937 and Talula's severe angina attack in 1939, they watched sadly while their home was torn up in 1940 to be remodeled for two apartments, though they were grateful that Burlie and his family would come live with them and let them have a new little cast-iron stove for their small kitchen. Talula's quilting frame had to be taken down and given to her daughter-in-law Alice. (The old frame with its denim strips still intact has been saved by Alice's daughter in Michigan.) During that difficult disruption of their accustomed space and habits, Talula's letters to Mollie Ruth increased to two or three a week.

Glittering Star V, *below right.* This 1930s *Glittering Star* quilt is one of several Talula made using plain pastel colors for sashing. She continued to piece *Glittering Star* blocks to use up her smallest scraps and left at her death enough blocks for her daughter-in-law Alice to make into two matching quilts for twin beds. *Below:* Detail of *Glittering Star.*

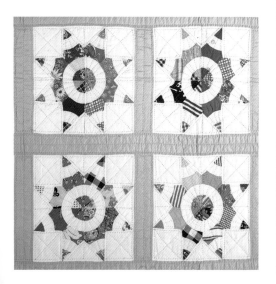

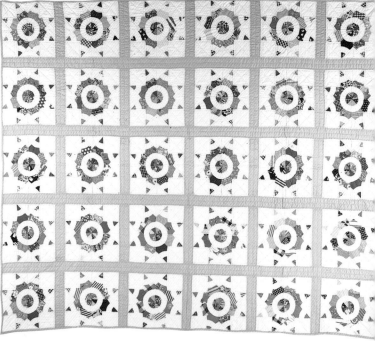

September 16, 1940:
Many, many thanks for the prints. They are pretty. You might go to the store and get 5 or 6 yards of the green for I may make several of those quilts . . . as I may want to make one for each of the children. Send 1/2 yard like the little dark piece . . . seems we can't get such pretty goods here. . . .

September 18, 1940:
I have got started on that pretty rug. . . . I trimmed it yesterday . . . that is the lining. . . . I will let it lay on the bed and work at it until I'm tired, and then rest while I work on the quilt. . . . I think I will start on the quilt today. . . .

September 25, 1940:
Yes! The package came and the material is pretty. I have the rug almost finished and am getting on fine with the quilt. . . .

September 30, 1940:
I have finished the rug and have one quilt finished. Got them finished Friday in time to start the other one. I want to finish it this week. . . .

October 2, 1940:
We have fixed the quilt and put in the rug as there was plenty of room in the box. . . . I am almost done with another quilt. P.S. Please don't send me anymore cloth as I have so much already. I have enough pieces cut for several tops, as I just keep on cutting pieces until I'd cut all I could get from pieces that was too small for the Grecian Star. Then I have a few more scraps and other cloth I've had for a long time. I want to get them all pieced up while I live and am able.

Tom in his handcrafted rocking chair, swaying gently back and forth as if tuned to the rhythms of the universe, was a familiar sight to family and passers by. He designed the chair with its comfortable foot rest and had his brother George Washington help him make it about 1895. (Its natural wood finish was not painted until long after his death.) Tom's health had been so eroded from severe bouts with malaria in his youth, he was never a truly well man and needed much rest. Talula and her daughters saw that indoors or out, Papa had a "nice place to rest." (Almira to Talula, May 1913).

Eight-point Star, c. 1938. One of several quilts of this design Talula could piece and put together in about a week, probably quilted by Beulah Clark in early 1950. Talula's eccentric use of stripes and a mixture of floral prints with some *Glittering Star* diamonds thrown in make what could be an ordinary quilt interesting, indeed.

"Crook," the good milk cow with the broken tail, whose life was saved by wrapping her in one of Talula's old worn quilts. She had been tied to a peach tree in the orchard to eat the grass that would otherwise go to waste; she had switched her tail against a beehive and had been stung all over. Later each sting abscessed, and swarms of flies made them worse when ointment was applied. Talula's quilt and socks made by Almira were the answer. The photo was taken at Glendale Farm, the home of Robert and Almira Butler about 1940 (courtesy, Ruth B. Potts).

These letters and many others that followed suggest Talula was piecing about one quilt a week and that she might, indeed, have left at her death one hundred quilt tops she made *during those last few years*. Tom took a growing interest in her work, occasionally choosing a quilt he liked so much he wanted to "have someone quilt it and he keep it." Their love and concern for each other was a beautiful thing to see; everyone who knew them with few exceptions saw these two old-fashioned folks as people apart, saintly and yet very much alive and down-to-earth. On winter days Talula sat by the fireplace in her little homemade, straight-back chair, cushioned with two or three pillows, piecing quilts. Her quilt closet nearby was filled with bags and boxes of scraps or cut pieces neatly arranged. A favorite cat teased her or lazed cozily on the hearth. Tommie listened intently to the news and made observations in his still-strong voice. When the sun was high in the sky, once a week Tom would take their feather bed out to air and sun it.

On warm summer days Talula would sit in her small rocking chair on the wide, shady veranda beside Tommie in his big one. She would have a Three Musketeers box on her lap, lifting off the little cut pieces with unbelievable speed and placing the finished squares in a basket beside her chair. As Tommie rocked and reminisced, she would rock and sew; and the memories of old times and places came back as vividly as yesterday.

Occasionally Tom would break out in a great deep laugh. Talula's face would light up with amusement and her shoulders shake with controlled mirth at remembering some funny thing; she had been taught "ladylike" manners so well by Analiza she never, after early childhood, was heard to laugh aloud, though often she would be so full of laughter her whole body would shake.

A Communication

I desire to let my friends know why I am not affiliated with any religious denomination. I have become very much discouraged with modern religion, because modern denominations, claiming to take the Bible and it alone as their guide, utterly refuse to practice certain truths taught therein. I believe that all those who claim to take the Bible and it alone as their guide are doing a very grave wrong when they fail to do so. It is a fearful thing to add to, or to take from, the truths taught in the scripture. I refer you to Rev. 22:18–19—also Deut. 4:2 and 12:32 and Prov. 30:6. These passages teach us the importance of doing just what the Bible teaches.

Just how such men as the great leaders in the Methodist and Presbyterian churches could be satisfied with sprinkling as Baptism is something that I am not able to understand, and there are thousands of men today, who call themselves ministers of the Gospel, who are doing all in their power to keep the people from believing the truth in regard to the Sabbath. They are teaching the people that the Fourth Commandment of the Decalogue was done away with or changed when Christ was crucified, when the Bible says plainly that all his Commandments are sure, they stand fast forever and ever (Psalms 111:7–8). They certainly do deny the plain truth. And how women who claim to take the Bible and it alone as their guide can stand up before a congregation called a Church and make a speech and have a clear conscience, is something I can not understand, when the Bible says plainly that it is a shame for them to do so (1st. Cor. 14:34–35). And Paul said he was not taught but by the revelation of Jesus Christ. (Gal. 1:12).

These are some of the reasons why I am not a member of any visible church, and I believe I am right in my views. Of course, I know my views are not popular, but I had rather be alone and be right with God than to be with the majority and be wrong. And the Bible certainly does sustain me in my views.

We should "earnestly contend for the faith which was once delivered unto the Saints" (Jude 3). "Remember therefore from whence thou art fallen, and repent, and do the first works; or else I will come unto thee quickly, and will remove thy candlestick out of his place, except thou repent" (Rev. 2:5). "Behold: to obey is better than sacrifice and to harken than the fat of rams" (1st Sam. 15:22). Strict obedience to His word is the only acceptable service man can render unto God.

Yours in the interest of truth,

—T. J. Bottoms, April 1941
Athens, Alabama.

Summer was the time for visiting; and as the seemingly endless stream of company came and went, Talula reported every detail to Mollie Ruth, delighted with the liveliness of the talk and tolerating the noise of grandchildren clattering up and down the bare stairs or romping on the veranda, all the time her hands busy with piecing. When the younger children came and stood by her chair, she would put her work down long enough to trot to the kitchen and open Elisa's old pie safe. Then she would make them their favorite snack, "syrup in a hole," by poking her finger into the end of a soft buttermilk biscuit and filling it with golden, home-made sorghum mo-

Glittering Star I, *right,* c. late 1800's. This unusual
pieced star pattern may have been originated by
Talula's mother-in-law Elisa McElroy Bottoms to use
up the smallest scraps left over from the other work.
The five alternating dark and light pieces in each of
the diamonds that make up the stars create a multi-
circular center and "glittering" points. Each twelve-
inch block utilizes from three to fifteen different
calicoes and solids. The blocks are joined by pieced
red-checked and green calico sashing. Filled with
thick, hand-carded cotton, it is finely quilted with
coarse, perhaps homespun thread, is expertly hand
bound in green, and has a manufactured one-piece
coarse muslin backing. This is the first of at least nine
Glittering Star quilts Talula made; she continued
making them possibly into the 1930's, and one was
left unquilted, showing her characteristic one-eighth
inch seams. The pieced sashing with small nine-patch
blocks at intersection points utilizes a checked
gingham and the same yellow-green calico found in so
many of Talula's quilts over a period of twenty-five
years; one is temped to guess she bought a whole bolt
of that fabric. *Below:* Detail of *Glittering Star* I.

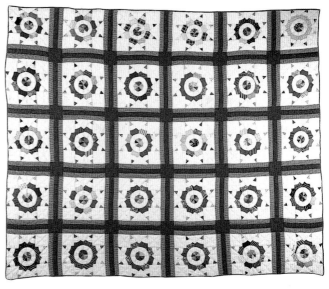

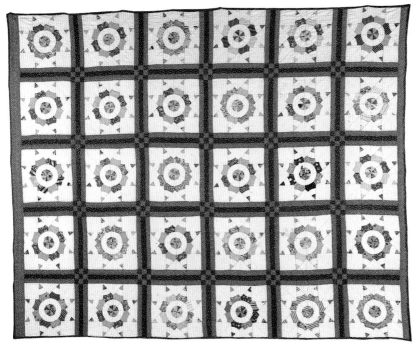

Glittering Star II. Fabrics in this quilt suggest it was made between 1900 and 1915 during the Cullman County years. Talula did not quilt it, and the unevenness of the quilting "in the ditch" suggests it may have been a "quilting-party" quilt.

lasses. "I never saw anyone who loved company more than Mama and Papa do," Mollie Ruth wrote in her journal in the early fall of 1941.

It had lifted their hearts when Mollie Ruth announced at Christmas 1939 she was taking a leave of absence from teaching to write the novel based on her parents' lives. She had been working on it piecemeal for several years and had decided to come home, build a little study in the orchard, and work there in solitude. But she had left her writing and gone back to Oklahoma when it became apparent the United States was preparing for war. Tom and Talula were listening intently to their radio when Secretary of the Navy Frank Knox, under the solemn eyes of President Franklin D. Roosevelt, reached into the big lottery barrel and drew the number to choose the first draftee for this new war. "His mother was there and she cried out, but when she went up to speak her heart was too full and she couldn't do it," Talula wrote to Mollie Ruth. Soon their own promising grandson would be called. Jim Ed, born just twenty years to the day after their son George, was near genius and a scientist like his Uncle Roger, but his was the eighth number to be drawn that day. By 1943 he would be missing in action in North Africa, and no trace of him or his P-38 fighter plane would ever be found.

Their daughter Almira's heavy grief was heartrending for the old parents, because it was silent and deep, full of denial and hope. They shared her grief with a compassion only those who have suffered everything can know and accepted the new loss with impervious faith. They remembered Almira's inexpressible joy when Jim Ed was baptized in the Paint Rock River that wound its way through his father's farm, and they knew they would soon cross over and meet their grandson "on the banks of the River of Life and clasp his glad hand of welcome."

Talula lived on for three more years until her death in 1946, and Tom died in 1947. They had been a little oasis of peace in the midst of a world torn by war. When it was time for them to go, several of their children rallied round and cared for them tenderly in their own little apartment until they loosed their hold on human life and quietly slipped away.

Tom and Talula Bottoms in front of Athens, Alabama, home about 1935. Having achieved another dream, the two old-fashioned people, never swayed by styles and trends, enjoyed their modest comforts and wanted nothing more. But within a few years they would relinquish their hard-earned independence, as well as any debt remaining on their home. They would have deeded all the land and the house itself to their children, would make the difficult adjustment to having their home torn up and remodeled into two apartments, and would happily "make the best of it." With fewer responsibilities, Talula could then indulge herself fully in her quilt work, which was the creative center and passion of her life.

CHAPTER 19

To Live or Die in Dixie

When Talula's daughter Mollie Ruth was drawn back to Fayette County in 1940 to complete research for her unpublished novel, *Taproots*, Margaret Mitchell had already become a celebrity overwhelmed by acclaim. The two women had met in July 1936 at a Blowing Rock, North Carolina, writers' workshop. Mollie Ruth had gone there from Oklahoma to learn, and Margaret Mitchell to hide from a clamoring public that frightened her by its fanatic eagerness to "touch the hem of the garment" of this woman who had become almost a saint overnight. She had given a depressed and hopeless nation the illusion of something to believe in, an antidote to despair and hopelessness.

Mollie Ruth was awed by the famous, shy little woman who sat in her hat and house dress as she spoke to the class almost in a whisper, and who kept her eyes closed when the group pictures were taken. She could hardly wait to get home and give her old parents her autographed copy of *Gone with the Wind* to read.

But Talula was too busy piecing quilts and didn't care to read it. "I don't like fixion very well. My good old father would never let us children read a novil. He didn't believe in anything but the truth," Talula wrote to her daughter in Oklahoma.[1]

Tom struggled through most of the thousand pages, frequently slamming the book down in disgust. "Of course a lot of it is true," he exclaimed, "but some of it is just lies! If she had to tell *everything*, why didn't she stick to the truth!" Then he and Talula would talk long hours while she pieced quilts, for there were scenes in the story that brought tears to his eyes, so vivid were the memories they revived.

Nannie Dickson's daughter Lela, who had courageously and with great sacrifice cared for her mother as Nannie's life fell apart in the early twenties, after her mother's death turned to her Aunt Lula for support. She was able to overcome much of her grief and remorse by visits for two decades to Athens and by frequent correspondence with Talula. From their niece Tom and Talula learned that Margaret Mitchell had asked Lela, whose parents had been close neighbors to her own Fitzgerald ancestors, to drive around Fayette and Clayton counties with her, to point out sites of this Civil War story. Tom and Talula thus knew before it was published an important book was being written about that sorrowful time. It would be a book that provided people not only entertainment and temporary escape from troubled times, but the hope that they, like Scarlett O'Hara, could become masters of their world, not victims.[2]

But there was another and more realistic escape for many women from the despair of those depression years. It had become fashionable again as in days almost forgotten, to use up dress scraps and buy new material to make those useful bed coverings, once available only by the work of women's hands. Doctors, too, at last had begun to recognize craftwork and quilting as healing therapy for people who despaired at the bleak outlook for their families in this once mighty nation that seemed so fallen now as the proud leader of democracy and prosperity in the world. Talula's own Dr. Belue had allowed her to work at piecing quilts when she could do nothing else after her increasingly severe angina attacks began in the late 1930s.

Margaret Mitchell and Mollie Ruth Bottoms at Writer's Colony, Blowing Rock, North Carolina in July 1936. Mollie Ruth is standing center in dark dress. Left to right sitting: Harold Blodgett, Herschell Brickell *(New York Post)*, Margaret Mitchell, Edwin Granberry *(New York Evening Sun)*. Margaret Mitchell who was "running away" from a clamoring public that frightened her, accepted Edwin Granberry's invitation to this quiet retreat, the summer campus of Rollins College (Florida) where he was professor of English, on condition that she would remain anonymous. After she arrived, she was persuaded to spend a couple of hours discussing her book with the other writers. (Photo from MRB papers.)

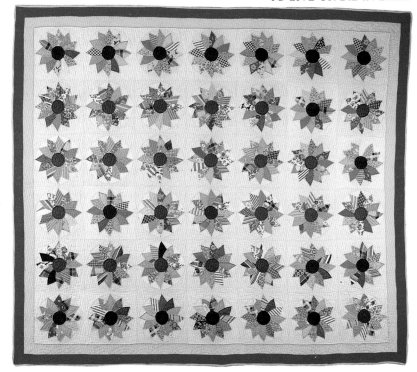

Sunflower I, c. 1940. The pattern for this pieced quilt may have come from Talula and Tom's Texas relatives. (A like quilt is shown in *The Quilters: Woman and Domestic Art,* an oral history by Patricia Cooper and Norma Bradley Buford.) Talula kept in close touch with her Texas relatives and saved many letters from them. (Quilted by Beulah Clark in the 1950s.)

Mollie Ruth never completed the second volume of her novel. She chose not, or could not bring herself, to write realistically about the life of her family after their move to Alabama from Georgia after she was born in 1901. Her father had not liked the frankness of volume one of *Taproots* and would not give his consent for her to pursue publication. She was crushed by his reaction, stricken by a "nervous breakdown" while she was trying to revise that first volume. After that, she put her novel away and wrote hundreds of sonnets, numerous book reviews, many poems and stories for children, and some fine articles for the *Christian Science Monitor's* "Home Forum," but not another line on her novel.

The talented Margaret Mitchell with her sweeping vision and remarkable grasp of history could never bring herself to write the sequel to her novel people demanded. Instead, she wrote thousands of eloquent letters, almost compulsively revealing herself as rarely confident, always romantic, and often beset by doubts, unable to gather her talents to write another novel.

Talula kept on quilting, and seemed always able to face reality no matter how stark, much as her grandmother Tabitha had done, and Talula lived almost as long. Tabitha Gilbert died in

1888 at the age of 85, Talula at age 84 in 1946. But Talula was unwilling to go to her rest without leaving her own written record of the nine decades in which she had lived. When Mollie Ruth's decision to publish her novel began to waver, Talula gathered up the notes she had given her daughter and sat down to write her own story. She pieced quilts until a few weeks before her death March 9, 1946. She was laid to rest in the family graveyard on the farm, and every day until Tom's death twenty-one months later, he walked the half mile to her grave taking fresh flowers or just his own deep thoughts.[3]

In 1895 John Gilbert added a codicil to his will entailing the property his son Joe was to receive as his legacy; he also revoked the item in his will that named Joe co-executor. Joe "worked himself to death" for "Railroad Business" in Atlanta, went through bankruptcy, moved to Cincinnati, and died of tuberculosis "in a little shack on the side of a hill" in 1926.[4]

"This has indeed been a cruel world to me," Joe wrote in a fine, delicate hand to Talula in 1915, still grieving over the death of his eleven-year-old son in 1911. "I sometimes wish I had gone, too, about the time I used to sit on the old back kitchen steps after the War and cry 'Oh, Lule, give me some bread.'"

Talula's step-mother, Analiza, died of tuberculosis in 1886 at age 49. John Gilbert, just twenty years to the day after his marriage to Analiza, and less than seven months after her death, married Analiza's sister, Mary.

Talula's half-sister Bettie, Analiza's only daughter, lived to be 87, indulged by a devoted and patient husband and surrounded by many children and grandchildren, few of whom moved from Fayette County. The large home on property she inherited from her father is now a restaurant.

John and Analiza Gilbert's youngest son, Brother Will to Talula, never married. He inherited the two homes his father had built (in 1851 and in 1884) and much other property. He allowed most of it to slip into hands outside the family who cared nothing for its dramatic history; so the property never became the legacy John Joseph Gilbert had intended. His and Holly Gilbert's home built in 1851, Talula's birthplace, was torn down in 1985 and the once-thriving farm is now the exclusive Oak Manor development of "executive" homes.

What is left of the comfortable, rambling house Tom, Talula, and their children built up so valiantly in Cullman County is easily recognizable today, though it stands a stark, crumbling skeleton of its former self against a barren landscape. The once proud veranda is gone and in its place is a low corrugated roof held up by sapling posts. But the same massive stones Tom put there in 1905 still serve as its front steps, while only one of the "three stone fireplaces" remains to tell the story of those years of toil and grit, self-sufficiency and courage. The present owner, a sweet, determined little lady in her eighties, refuses to leave the old house which has been her home for fifty years, while her son and his wife, Logan's postmistress, live nearby in their modern brick ranch-style home.

The hamlet of Logan today little resembles the frontier village of 1900. A new brick post office rests on the site of the old gin where Tom once took his cotton in the fall. An abandoned building, once a general store and before that a blacksmith shop, stands starkly on one corner of the crossroads. The little Rabbit Hutch restaurant which "opens on Friday, Saturday and Sunday evenin's at five o'clock" for food and camaraderie, seems an anachronism when viewed from the steps of the imposing new Methodist church across the way and from the Baptist church with its own tennis courts a hundred yards down the road. Both churches have grown from the small frame structures that nourished the spiritual life of Logan's frontier people although the soil on that area of Brindley Mountain is "so pore nothing can be grown on it."[4]

Tom and Talula's Limestone County home is today much altered and in the hands of people who know little if any of its history. The farm itself, now a suburb of Athens, Alabama, is a development of executive homes whose owners will move on with their next promotion. The old James Bottoms farm in Fayette County, Georgia, Tom and Talula's first home, was sold years ago to developers who turned it into the County Greens Golf Course beside Morning Creek. The only record that remains of the drama of courage and survival of those years besides Elisa and Talula Bottoms's quilts, is Talula's Memoir, and the old letters and records dating back to 1821 that she and Tom had saved.

More than one hundred of Talula's quilts remain today in the hands of her descendants (scattered from New York to California), the loving legacy of a courageous woman who will not be forgotten.

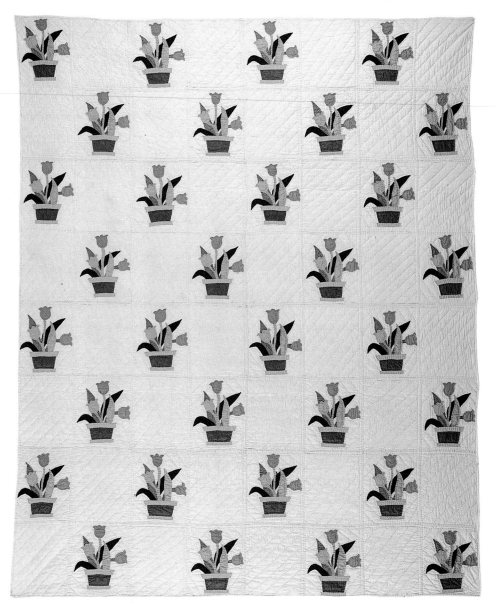

Tulip, above, c. 1930s. Made for son Burlie and daughter-in-law Alice, and quilted by Alice in 1940s or 1950s. No pattern source has been found for this unusual quilt. *Right:* Detail of *Tulip.*

Afterword

If there is one thing to be learned from Talula and Tom Bottoms's story it is that there were people in the South who did not waste time and energy after the War on bitter resentment toward the "Yankee Devils" who had plundered their good land and decimated their families. Instead—and there doubtless were thousands like them—the Gilberts and Bottoms were grateful to have survived and diligently set their hands and hearts to the task of rebuilding. They overcame grief and loss of loved ones through hard work, tilling the soil, and making the best use of what could be salvaged from the destruction. Necessity required resourcefulness, a community spirit of concern, and sharing with neighbors—qualities that became lifelong virtues.

Dismissing as foolhardy the resistance of their fellow Georgians who controlled the state and delayed its readmission to the Union until 1870, these families promptly renewed their commitment to the re-United States. Innumerable hard-working farmers and tradesmen had innocently, without hatred, simply obeyed the laws of *their* land and gone along with that "rich planters' war." With either a few or no slaves, they had lived self-sufficient lives, close to the land and in tune with the rhythms of nature; at War's end they were thankful the land would again yield its abundance to sustain them and their children.

There had been no more patriotic people in the whole country than those simple farmers in Georgia before the War, though many would be driven by the evils of Reconstruction to become radicals and "Red-necks." They had learned well, even with their scant education in log schoolhouses, the sacrifices made by the architects of the new republic dedicated to freedom and equality. Many had even named their sons for those great leaders.

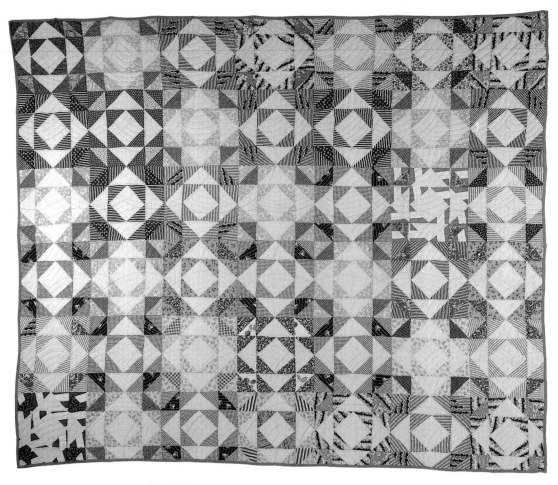

Bettie's Scrap Quilt is an example of the many scrap quilts Talula made for her children's families to use for everyday cover. Her great-grandchildren later took some of them to college and untold numbers were finally worn to shreds and discarded.

Three of James and Elisa Bottoms's six sons had been named for great men; their neighbors had done likewise. Identified with such men as George Washington, Thomas Jefferson, and James Madison, how could they do other than honor those men in their own lives? George Washington Bottoms promptly signed his Oath of Allegiance and was released from prison at Point Lookout, Maryland, in June 1865, grateful the War was over and that he would be allowed to take an old Confederate mule back to Georgia.

If Thomas Jefferson and Talula Bottoms ever wavered in their patriotic devotion to their country, even in 1918 when their son George's mutilated body was sent home from Camp Wheeler so shockingly stuffed into that small casket, it appears only by inference in the record. Their son Matt (named for his uncle, James Madison) was the only one articulate and tactful

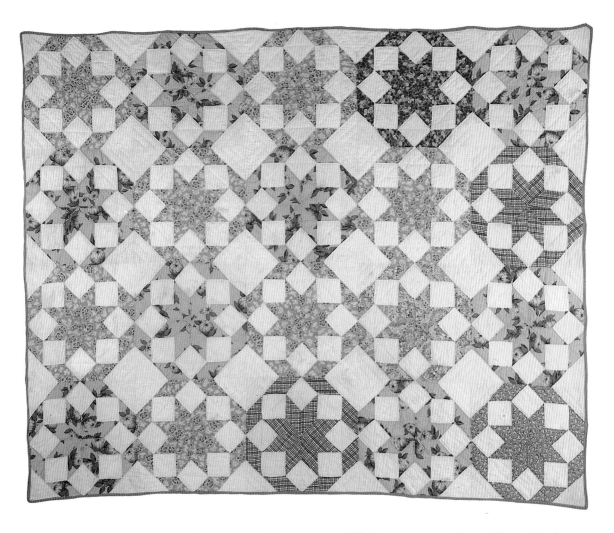

enough to write letters of inquiry and protest to Washington. Despite their carefully worded diplomacy, a few of Matt's letters suggest the family felt betrayed by the government to which they were so faithful, but they did not dwell on it long. They turned to the work of their hands and did what needed to be done: Tom's cotton farming, Talula's gardening, her chickens and her quilting. In these practical pursuits they dissolved their grief and confused feelings.

This book undermines the "Magnolia Myth" of the antebellum South that persists even today, not only in the North but among many Southerners and in the world at large. The Bottoms, the Gilberts, and the Fitzgeralds represent three "levels" of what might be termed the ordinary people of the old South, as distinguished from the legendary aristocracy of

Star and Chain. This late-nineteenth-century quilt is one Talula mentions in a letter to Mollie Ruth September 1940, as "not as pretty as the others," referring to the old pretty quilts she made in the 1880s and quilted in the 1890s. It shows hard times in that the plain white used to complete the blocks is of various fabrics—homespun, ribbed, muslin, and so forth. Completely handmade, except for binding, and nicely quilted, it is backed with coarse, "store-bought" muslin all in one piece. After hard use and many washings, the bold prints still hold their color, and the cotton batting remains intact, soft and as easy to quilt through as today's polyester.

marble-pillared mansions—plantations run by masters with hundreds of slaves—whose families lived in manorial splendor and educated their gentleman sons and spoiled "southern belle" daughters for lives of leisure.[1] The film version of *Gone with the Wind* perpetuates that myth, though Margaret Mitchell's novel describes Tara (the Fitzgerald place) as a rather plain, unpretentious house in contrast to the Wilkes's impressive mansion.[2] Even the O'Haras (the Fitzgeralds) were exceptions to the vast majority of hard-working southern people. *Legacy* represents that majority.

The story dispels also the myth of the South made up of a lazy or subservient population. It depicts a sturdy, hard-working family—of which there were many—at a time when "standard of living" was not in the vocabulary of the nation. How can we look back and feel sorry for those who with scant or modest means built their own houses, treated each hard circumstance as commonplace, considered many children a blessing, knew the joy of work and self-sufficiency, and created with their own hands those essential and often beautiful things they used and enjoyed? By their cheerfulness and integrity, their skills and resourcefulness, they transmitted respect for that way of life to their children, who felt valued by the work they contributed to the family's livelihood. Alas, that pattern would be broken in the next generation by a world which offered a mixed blessing of opportunity and material values.

Although the "book" education of Tom and Talula's children was often delayed until they were in their twenties before they finished high school, if they finished at all, it was that early training of the Bottoms children at home—their hardships notwithstanding—that determined an upright life, good citizenship, and success. All of their children led lives of integrity and service. Some were remarkably successful; most were resourceful enough, if necessity required, to make or grow whatever they needed that was not readily available as long as they lived.

Theirs was a far different world from today's in which standard of living is so much emphasized and work with the hands so undervalued. Yet today, the artifacts symbolic of those strong, simple people and their self-reliant way of life are becoming increasingly valuable and sought after; in 1987 an old handmade quilt sold in New York for $172,000.[3] Can it be that we still yearn for something essential to health and happiness left behind in the modern world of technology where the things we use and enjoy are more and more removed from the work of our hands? With obsolescence so built into the economy, beauty left behind for a fleeting utility, how exactly opposite is the world our children know from that in which our grandparents lived! Small wonder that we look with awe and nostalgia on the old handcrafted things and that the craft movement itself is a growing phenomenon.

Little needs to be said about the strong threads of simple faith and integrity that weave Tom and Talula's story together. In a sense, one could say they lived in a time before God and Nature—the supernatural and the natural—had been separated resulting in such bizarre manifestations of religion as that depicted in the world of Flannery O'Connor's stories of "good country people."

Though we cannot go back to Talula and Tom's unsophisticated, innocent faith or to their simple world, it was nevertheless a faith that had not been so corrupted as to make a mockery of religion. Perhaps there is still much we can learn from the way they looked at life. They *knew* a loving God was in control, for they had experiences to prove it—despite the inevitable hardships and unexplainable tragedies of their lives. Tom Bottoms's allegiance was finally to that God alone as the sun went down on his strong and simple life. His writings and the family records he left are not learned treatises on the meaning of life or the relation between God and man, but with most of his handcrafted inventions and household articles sold at auction in 1947, his words and those records remain his primary legacy.

Of all the artifacts, letters, and family documents Talula and Tom Bottoms saved (they span more than a century of turbulent American history), Talula's quilts, and those of her "mothers" before her, are the most tangible evidence of those years. Their needlework does not reflect oppressed women who felt like slaves in their own households. Instead, they show how women, in spite of their hard and often short lives, found their own quiet liberation in creative work—work that also gave comfort and joy to others. Talula lived at a time when a woman was a full partner with her husband in providing for the family. Indeed, her chicken yard and garden fed them in all kinds of weather, in good times and bad. Her butter, eggs, and chickens were as often traded for staples, for cloth to make clothes and quilts, as they were used at home. Her husband's cotton could be sold only once a year, and then most of the earnings were spent in settling year-long accounts to local merchants.

Detail of *Star and Chain*.

Talula's more than one hundred existing quilts are an unusual record of fabrics and quilt patterns in use in the South of those times. Because she was not especially affected by "quilt revivals," or by fad and fashion "doing that which is fashionable at the time rather than that which is reasonable,"[4] her quilts show what was available to a resourceful woman with a fine aesthetic sense and with only modest means at her disposal. Unself-consciously devoted to that lifelong creative passion, Talula made and treasured several of those exquisitely quilted "best" quilts—rarely used and expected to be saved and passed on as heirlooms—yet it is the predominance of her pieced quilts that reflect most vividly her life and times. Her scrap quilts, like those of her mother-in-law Elisa's, show astonishing thrift and ingenuity, as well as her realization of the value of time.

Regardless of crop failures, bad weather, hard times, children underfoot, deaths of loved ones, even their own ill health, women could pick up their scrapbags and sewing baskets and

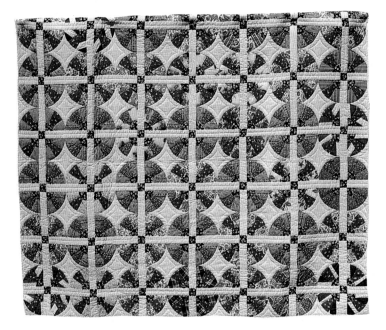

Samples of Talula's unfinished work.

work on their quilt blocks whenever they had spare moments. It was a serene and calming occupation, their hands were never idle, and the beauty they created from the chaos of old clothes and scraps gave a touch of elegance to otherwise plain, often drab, households. In addition, "the quilt allowed a woman the chance to assemble a lifetime of observation and experience in a tightly organized sharp-edged arrangement, soul-satisfying in its clear-cut precision and logical predictability," to quote Elisabeth Garrett in her Foreword to *Stitches in Time*.[5] With life so unpredictable, so fleeting, this work of their hands was the link between those dear ones soon to go or long gone and a generation yet unborn. Such work gave meaning and purpose to their lives. All one has to do today to sense that link and that meaning is to touch and look ever so closely at an old handmade quilt.

In her quiltmaking, Talula, like innumerable women of her time, found meaning in the stewardship both of her household and of the resources the earth made abundantly available. Both required diligence, hard work, and efficient use of everything, which became lifelong habits. For a very long time following the Civil War, such women of the South prepared everything they needed to make those comfortable coverings for their families. How different from many women today whose work out-

Grandmother's Fan, left, c. 1940s. This quilt appears to have four of the little fan squares put together with points toward the corners, the 10½-inch squares then joined by lattice strips; yet it is just the opposite. The pattern is an unequal nine-patch with points of fans facing center to form a circular pattern intersected by a cross. Talula left many unquilted tops like this that were made in her final years with wider seams and longer stitches, perhaps using bundles of scraps she is known to have ordered. At least five of them have the same yellow background and cross, and in some the blocks are sewn together by a sewing machine. At least two of these quilts, and perhaps more, were left in stacks of the little hand-sewn fan blocks, and joined into quilt tops later. In the early 1950s, Talula's daughter Almira was "very busy making and having made quilts that Grandma Bottoms pieced for her." (R. L. Butler to daughter Nancilu, March 1950). At that time she sent a dozen or more tops—at least five of them like this—to others: to her brother Gilbert and to nieces and nephews. Some she gave to her own children after having had them quilted by Beulah Clark (now Webb) who lived in a log cabin on Glendale Farm and charged $8 per quilt for her work.

side the home provides merely money to buy things that are soon discarded, things not valued because the work of loving and creative hands has not been invested in them.

An Indian woman exactly describes the sane and healing function of the hands-on work of quiltmaking as well as the value so conferred, even though she speaks of India's indigenous crafts. "The human touch does something to the fragments which are brought together in the finished piece where they mingle and cling together, drawn by the magnetism of love, as if seeking one another, to give birth to a new life in fresh form—unlike the tumult and pressuring of a powerful machine where the pieces seem helpless and lost."[6]

It is no wonder Talula (and finally her daughters and granddaughters) saved so many of her own as well as her mother-in-law's old scrap quilts. Even today those quilts carry in their soft and ingeniously hand-pieced texture the aura of love invested in them by those quiet, devoted women who survived difficulties hard for us to imagine. Unknowingly, they performed the function of artists—making something *useful* and *beautiful*. With no dreams of personal glory, they lost themselves in absorbing work and were thus "transformed into artists. Greater opportunity to live in intimacy with beauty should not be the privilege of the few, but the inheritance of all," Kamaladevi says. Is it possible that Talula's legacy, those insights so vividly expressed in Kamaladevi's words, can be our legacy, too? Her quilts and her story are evidence they can.

Notes

Chapter 2: *The War in Fayette County*

1. *The History of Fayette County, 1821–1971* (Fayetteville, Georgia: Fayette County Historical Society, 1977), p. 133.

2. Ibid, p. 366.

3. Ibid.

4. This story, told in 1987 to the writer by Frances Dixon Davies, a Fayetteville native who knew "Miss Anna" personally, was recorded in 1940 by Mollie Ruth Bottoms in an interview with her great Aunt Susannah Marshbourne's daughter, Mary Thornton.

5. Talula Gilbert Bottoms, Memoir (privately published by Nancilu B. Burdick in 1983 as "Autobiography of Talula Gilbert Bottoms" and distributed largely to Talula's grandchildren), p. 12.

Chapter 3: *Broken Families*

1. Interview notes: M. R. Bottoms with her father, T. J. Bottoms, Athens, Alabama, 1940.

2. Ibid.

3. Anne Edwards, *Road to Tara: The Life of Margaret Mitchell* (New Haven and New York: Technor and Fields, 1983), p. 27.

4. Ibid., p. 139.

5. Ibid., pp. 26–27.

6. T. Bottoms, Memoir, pp. 19–20.

7. Ibid., p. 12.

8. Ibid., p. 43.

Chapter 4: *Wounded Women*

1. M. R. Bottoms, Interview notes.

2. T. Bottoms, Memoir, p. 21.

3. Ibid., pp. 46–47. "My stepmother . . . said my mother had made a nice quilt for all of her children but one, so I was going to be left out, but one of my brothers died a young man . . . so I got the quilt of my mother's that was to go to Mat." There was some disagreement about the *Orange Bud* quilt. This was the quilt that should have gone to Talula, according to her Grandmother Tabitha, but it went to Analiza's only daughter instead. Talula then made an *Orange Bud* quilt like her mother's for herself, "quilted it nicely" and later gave it to her oldest son, Ary. That quilt has since been lost or worn out.

Chapter 5: *Healing*

1. T. Bottoms, Memoir, p. 127.

2. M. R. Bottoms, Interview notes with parents, 1940.

3. Talula Bottoms, notes she called "My Life and Reminiscences from My Earliest Remembrance" made between 1934 and 1940.

Chapter 6: *Amazing Grace*

1. T. Bottoms, Memoir, p. 8–9.

2. Ibid., pp. 83–84.

3. Ibid.

4. *The Baptist Hymn Book: 1000 Hymns of Praise* (Philadelphia: American Baptist Publishing Society, 1871). Printed with words only, no musical scores, to be sung "on a credit," that is, like a call and a response, the preacher or leader speaking the words and the congregation following in song. No books were needed using this method; indeed, many in the congregation could not read.

Chapter 7: *Hesitation*

1. T. Bottoms, Memoir, pp. 9–10.

2. M. R. Bottoms, Interview with parents, 1940.

Chapter 8: *Awakening*

1. *The History of Fayette County*, p. 722; T. Bottoms, Memoir, p. 86.

2. T. Bottoms, Memoir pp. 14, 43.

3. T. Bottoms, written in pencil on rough tablet paper, c. 1870s, when Talula was twelve or thirteen.

4. Undated letter written in child's scrawl before Minta developed her characteristically beautiful handwriting. Preserves were reserved for company, and the milk was saved to sour and churn for butter, a precious commodity needed for barter.

Chapter 9: *Realization*

1. Opera flannel was a lightweight variety of highly finished wool flannel, first made in Massachusetts in 1860, piece-dyed in fancy colors, originally intended for opera cloaks, "especially adapted . . . for women's house sacques." This information courtesy Joan Stephens of Potomac, Maryland who found it at the Smithsonian Institution; T. Bottoms, Memoir, p. 63.

2. T. Bottoms, Memoir, p. 171.

3. Burdick interview with Sarah Bottoms Barber, October 1984.

Chapter 11: *On Jordan's Stormy Banks*

1. Letter, Cathern Allen to T. Bottoms, September 15, 1891.

2. T. Bottoms, notes.

3. Talula kept trying to get an education until she was grown. A letter saved from a much-loved teacher, Miss Julia Smarr, shows Talula went to school at fifteen and had many friends. John Gilbert was still balancing attendance records in 1880 for the Gilbert Schoolhouse on unused pages of his old Civil War Record Book. Talula, at eighteen, was one of the pupils; her time in school from January 5 to May 14 is shown as fifty-one full days and four half-days at eight and three-quarter cents per day, costing her father $4.63 and ¾ cents for that term. Her half-sister, Bettie, five years younger, spent eighty-seven days in school. John Gilbert had six children, ages six to twenty, in school that term, and all the others attended more regularly than Talula. Miss Smarr boarded with the Gilberts that year and gave a sacred song book to Talula and a picture of herself to Talula's brother Joe.

4. John Joseph Gilbert's will dated 1893, probated in Jonesboro, GA. in 1906.

5. M. R. Bottoms, Interview notes, 1940. Elisa would not drink this folk remedy (tea made by boiling rich pine knots) for influenza. All the rest drank it and recovered.

6. Ibid.

Chapter 12: *Decision*

1. Letter, Cathern Allen to T. Bottoms, September 1891.

2. When her son Robert Hampton Bottoms died after having become paralyzed, the doctors were puzzled and wanted to do an autopsy. Elisa would not allow his body to be used in a way she considered desecration. After he was buried in the family graveyard, the family heard rumors that some local boys planned to rob his grave and sell his body for a large sum of money. For a month or longer, Tom and George took turns sleeping beside their brother's grave with their hound dog, Roud, to alert them. The family believed it was a fish bone he had swallowed years before that had made its way to his brain.

3. Tom had been ordained to preach sometime before this incident. He had desperately wanted to take a year of study at Emory College, had tried to get assistance from the Baptist Association by writing to Rev. A. C. Smith; because of his age, his financial condition, and his family responsibilities, he was turned down.

4. Dr. George Wallis, letter to Tom Bottoms, May 14, 1902. Wallis makes a fervent plea ("speaking for all who know you here") for Tom to return to Fayette County; his letter is a glowing tribute to this man of integrity, whose godly influence Wallis felt was sorely needed in that county.

Chapter 13: *Upheaval*

1. General Logan, named "Black Jack Logan" by the volunteer Union regiment he commanded in the Vicksburg and Atlanta Campaigns, after the War helped organize the Grand Army of the Republic. He was strongly supportive of President Andrew Johnson's lenient policies toward the South and is credited also with originating the idea of Memorial Day in 1868 (Margaret Jean Jones, *Combing Cullman County*, Cullman, Alabama: Modernistic Printers, 1972, p. 80).

2. Tom and his mother had the old sawmill to dispose of after it failed. After selling it to a man who "never paid a cent on it," Tom traded it for a house in Jonesboro, then sold that for $600 without telling Talula and put the money away to save for a farm of his own.

3. T. Bottoms, Memoir, p. 118.

4. Letter, Mollie Bottoms to T. Bottoms, February 20, 1899. Mollie's regular letters through June 1928 report in minute and sometimes gruesome detail the events and the comings and goings of innumerable people in Fayette County. They constitute an unusual folk history of that time and place.

5. M. R. Bottoms, Interview notes, 1941.

6. The old log "Gurley" schoolhouse and its successor, the first Walker Schoolhouse in the county, were described for Mollie Ruth by an older brother, Emmett, in 1941 while she was writing her unpublished novel, *Taproots*.

Chapter 14: *Return and Farewell*

1. Letter, T. Bottoms to T. J. Bottoms, December 28, 1901.

2. Letter, T. J. Bottoms to T. Bottoms, July 29, 1906.

3. Robert P. Tristram Coffin in his poem, "Crystal Moment" from *Collected Poems* (New York: The Macmillan Company, 1932; published in *Poetry I*, The Macmillan Co. 1962), p. 80. Mollie Ruth carried on a lengthy correspondence with Mr. Coffin who urged her to pursue publication of *Taproots*.

4. Letter, Bettie Gilbert Stell to T. Bottoms, Aug. 15, 1907.

5. Letter, Mollie Bottoms to T. Bottoms, February 28, 1927.

Chapter 15: *Broken Circles*

1. T. Bottoms, Memoir, p. 130.

2. David Mattison Bottoms ("a kind and tender hearted brother") to his sister Almira, October 13, 1913; T. Bottoms to Claude Bottoms, March 24, 1914.

3. Population of Cullman County in 1890 was "white: 13,439, colored: 38. In 1900, 17,849 (white)." L. D. Miller, *History of Alabama* (Birmingham, AL, 1901). This volume was a textbook Almira used at Jacksonville State Normal (College) in 1911.

4. Tom's brother George and nephews Jim and Claude Bottoms sent periodic reports that both house and land were being abused, allowed to run down, stripped of timber. Their old home place was sold in haste and quite blindly by Tom for Talula in February 1913, and unknowingly to a man "of no morals." "When we think of the old place around which so many tender memories were twined, it makes us sad and sorry it has fallen into such hands . . ." Letter, Claude Bottoms to Rev. Thomas Bottoms, February 19, 1913.

5. Letter, Mary J. Hand (Popular, Montana) to Mrs. T. J. Bottoms, October 12, 1913. The second attempt was in the late thirties. See *Uncoverings 1984*, p. 23. Talula donated three quilts to raffle for purchase of land to build a community church.

6. Letter, T. Bottoms to Claude Bottoms, March 24, 1914, enclosing copies of Almira's correspondence with the man in question. Talula, to "save the daughter we love so dearly," had violated her own conscience and invaded the privacy of her daughter's letter box.

7. Letter, T. Bottoms to "My Dear Children at Battle Creek," June 7, 1914.

8. Letter, D. M. Bottoms to oldest brother, A. T. Bottoms, with enclosures, February 4, 1918. When Tom insisted the local undertaker open the casket for himself and his oldest sons, their grief was compounded by incredulity and anger, their patriotic spirit shaken to its foundation. They discovered the shocking condition of the autopsied body, but could not complain or question the War Department, for it would expose the violation by their undertaker and friend of opening the casket.

Chapter 16: *Triumph and Letting Go*
1. Several letters from customers ordering his seed, including one from J. E. Matthews for "12 or 15 bushels." Alabama and Florida Agricultural Experiment Stations were testing and recommending it (Letters, Alabama Polytechnic Institute, February 25, 1925; University of Florida, January 13, 1926, and others).

2. Ruth E. Finley, *Old Patchwork Quilts and the Women Who Made Them* (Newton Center, Massachusetts: Charles T. Branford, 1983), p. 196.

3. Ibid.

4. John Naisbett, *Megatrends* (New York: Warner Books, 1984), pp. 45–46.

5. T. Bottoms, Memoir, pp. 115, 203.

6. Robert Giroux, Introduction, *Flannery O'Connor, The Complete Stories* (New York: Farrar, Straus and Giroux, 1979).

7. Letter, O. W. Clark to Rep. Ed B. Almon, February 27, 1931. The Veterans Administration would not honor an affidavit from Dr. Wallis in Fayetteville, attending physician at George's birth in 1896, and their good friend who had married Talula's cousin. Their last resort was to go through their State Representative.

8. M. R. Bottoms, interviews with Almira B. Butler, 1938–39. Thrash was a severe fungus infection of mouth and upper digestive tract.

9. Letters from Robert Frost to M. R. Bottoms, February 10 to May 18, 1939, and copies of letters from M.R.B. to Robert Frost, December 1938—May 21, 1939. Robert Frost charged $500.00 for his 24-hour visit to Edmond College, $50 of which he later returned to reimburse M.R.B.'s Poetry Club treasury for free admission for students who could not afford the admission fee.

10. M. R. Bottoms, interview with her father, 1940.

11. Letter, R. R. Bottoms to mother and father, undated, probably 1915 or 1916. Roger graduated from Battle Creek (Michigan) High School in 1915. He was twenty-five.

12. Letter, R. R. Bottoms to "homefolks," February 2, 1918. Roger spent a year in Cuba where he developed the synthetic menthol largely used in medicines and drugs today. A partial list of his discoveries can be found in his sister Almira's genealogy, *Bottoms Families in America and Descendants*, 1963.

Chapter 17: *The Quilter*
1. Claude's text is from Revelation 14:13.

2. Letter, M. R. Bottoms to T. Bottoms, spring, 1934. Mollie Ruth had read *Lamb in His Bosom*, by Caroline Miller (New York: Harper and Row, 1933), a novel of pioneer life in Georgia that had just won the Pulitzer Prize. In 1936 she would read a more

famous novel, *Gone With the Wind,* and become even more excited about writing her own novel.

3. Note in Talula's writing on top of cardboard box where this and other letters were found three years after her daughter Almira's death in 1980.

4. Letter, T. Bottoms to "My Dear Children and Grandchildren in the U.S.," October 22, 1934.

5. Letter, T. Bottoms to M. R. Bottoms, January 26, 1935. The Townsend Plan was an idealistic proposal that would purportedly relieve starvation among people over sixty and boost the economy by requiring money distributed be spent within a month. It was proposed by Dr. Francis E. Townsend and was to be funded by a two per cent federal sales tax. Talula seems to have recognized it as so much talk.

6. Letter, M. R. Bottoms to T. Bottoms, October 6, 1935.

7. Letter, M. R. Bottoms to T. Bottoms, October 12, 1935.

8. According to legend, drinking from the sacred spring of the Greek god Apollo at Delphi, Greece, restored powers of creative expression.

9. Dorothy Frager, *The Book of Sampler Quilts,* (Radnor, Pennsylvania: Chilton Book Co., 1983), p. 94. The quilt is a complex variation of the eight-pointed star; a flower with gathered petals is pieced into the center of the arrowhead shaped diamonds. See also back page of *Quilter's Newsletter* Magazine, September 1980. Talula's quilt was put together without sash as this one was.

10. Lucille Hilty, "A Passion for Quiltmaking" in *Uncoverings, 1980,* ed. Sally Garoutte (Mill Valley, California: American Quilt Study Group, 1981), p. 15.

11. Letter, Mary McFarland (daughter of Talula's sister Bettie) to T. Bottoms, February 14, 1941.

12. Pattern #5531 ordered for ten cents from Woman's Service Bureau, Nashville *Banner,* February 18, 1936.

Chapter 18: *Fulfillment*

1. The doctors decided his paralysis of one side was caused by "bad teeth." Several abscessed, so all his teeth were pulled. He would never get a plate but lived on—toothless—his beard an adequate camouflage.

2. Burdick interview with Lillian Talula Bottoms Bee, March 1986.

Chapter 19: *To Live or Die in Dixie*

1. Letter, T. Bottoms to M. R. Bottoms, December 11, 1944, courtesy of Mary Bottoms Wentworth.

2. Edwards, p. 247.

3. Burdick, interview with Mrs. Gladie Coffman, who rented the tenant house on the Bottoms farm, July 1984.

4. Letter, Matt Bottoms to Talula Bottoms, March 1924; Joe Gilbert to Will Gilbert, 1926.

5. Interview with Jennie Tucker Puckett, October, 1987. Jennie has lived in Logan all of her ninety-two years and was well acquainted with Tom and Talula's children. She lives in the large two-story frame house once the dormitory of "Logan College," a short-lived institution that boarded students and educated them for $1 a month for primary students; $1.50 for intermediates; $2 for high school and college. All students were assessed ten cents a month for incidentals (Jones, *Combing Cullman County*).

Afterword

1. Talula's hard life in childhood and youth, like many of the misfortunes in anyone's life, proved a blessing. She was not a "southern belle" and therefore learned early not to be a romantic dreamer who would later be subject to painful disillusionment. She learned to take responsibility for her own circumstances, thus avoiding the destructive emotions of self-pity, blame, and manipulation.

2. The Wilkes plantation of the novel has long been understood by local people to be modeled on the old Crawford estate near Lovejoy, Georgia. That home is now owned by Betty Talmadge who bought the Tara facade used in filming *Gone with the Wind,* as well as the old Fitzgerald home, and moved them to her property. She had plans to establish a tourist attraction, but politics intervened. Rumor now has it a tourist *(Gone with the Wind)* site is being planned for neighboring Coweta County.

3. Robert Bishop, Director of Museum of American Folk Art, New York, speaking to a group of quilters at Huntsville Museum of Art, Huntsville, Alabama, March 1987.

4. John Rice Irwin, *A People and Their Quilts* (Exton, Pennsylvania: Schiffer Publishing Ltd., 1983), p. 130.

5. Elisabeth Donaghy Garrett in Foreword to *Stitches in Time: A Legacy of Ozark Quilts* (Rogers, Arkansas: Rogers Historical Museum, 1983).

6. Kamaladevi Chattapadhyaya in Introduction to *India: Village Tribal, Ritual Arts,* exhibit catalog to travelling exhibition (La Jolla, California: Mingei International, 1981), p. 8.

Appendix

Patterns known to have been used by Talula Bottoms

Quilt Name	Approximate Dates	Number of Quilts	Quilt Name	Approximate Dates	Number of Quilts
Autumn Leaf	(1890–1910)	1	Honey Bee	(1890–1910)	1
Baby Bunting	(1880s)	1	Improved Nine Patch	(1940s)	6
*Basket of Flowers	(1883–1900)	1	Ivy Basket	(unknown)	1
Bear Paw	1920–1935)	2	LeMoyne Star	(1890–1910)	1
Butterfly	1920–1935)	1	*Lifeboat	(1935)	2
Blue Birds in Easy Appliqué	(1936)	1	Lone Star	(1927–1929)	2
Carpenter's Wheel (Star with Diamonds)	(1890–1900)	3	*Orange Bud	(late 1800s)	1
			*Pear Basket	(1885–1900)	1
Caesar's Crown (Full-Blown Tulip)	(1900–1920)	1	Pink Piney (and Purple Piney)	(1930s)	2
*Colonial Girl	(1930s)	3	Pinwheel	(1920–1930)	1
Crazy (embroidered: silk, velvet, wool top)	(1890s)	1	Pot of Tulips	(1930s)	1
			Princess Feather	(1936–37)	1
			Priscilla	(1910–1920)	1
Crazy (utility: tied wool top and wool filled)	(1925–1935)	1	Queen's Parasol	1930s	1
			*Road to Texas	(late 1800s)	1
*Dahlia	(1930–1940)	2	*Rocky Mountain	(1880s)	1
Double Wedding Ring	(1930s)	3	Rocky Road to Kansas	(1930s)	2
Dutch Doll	(1928–1938)	5/6	Shoo-Fly	(1900–1920)	1
Eastern Star	(late 1800s)	1	Star (unnamed)	(1920s)	2
Eight-Point Star	(1935–1945)	4	*Star and Chain	(late 1800s)	1
Fancy Dresden Plate	(1930s)	4	Star of Bethlehem	(1890–1910)	1
*Feather	(1885)	1	Star of Many Points	(1900–1920)	1
Garden Bouquet	(1930s)	5	Sunbonnet Sue	(1930s)	2/3
*Glittering Star	(1880s–1930s)	9	Sunflower	(1935–1945)	10
Goose Tracks	(1880s–1930s)	3	Tulip Basket	(1930s)	2
Grandmother's Fan	(1940s)	8	Twelve-Point Star	(1920–1940)	4
*Grecian Star	(1940s)	10	Unnamed Scrap	(1910–1930)	3
			Variable Star	(1900–1925)	2

*Quilts mentioned in Talula's Memoir or letters.

Bibliography

Abbott, Shirley. *Womanfolks: Growing Up Down South*. New Haven and New York: Ticknor & Fields, 1983.

Bank, Mirra. *Anonymous Was a Woman*. New York: St. Martin's Press, 1979.

Baptist Hymn Book: 1000 Hymns of Praise. Philadelphia: American Baptist Publishing Society, 1871.

Bottoms, Mollie Ruth. *Taproots*. Unpublished manuscript written 1943.

————. Interview notes with parents, Athens, Alabama, 1940.

————. Personal papers and unpublished notes.

Bottoms, Talula. Memoir written in 1943, privately published as *Autobiography of Talula Gilbert Bottoms* by Nancilu Burdick, Orchard Park, New York, 1983.

Burdick, Nancilu B., "Talula Bottoms and her Quilts," in *Uncoverings 1984*, Sally Garoutte, ed. Mill Valley, California: American Quilt Study Group, 1985.

Butler, Almira B. *Bottoms Families in America and Descendants*. Privately published, 1962.

Cale, George S. *Cale's Encyclopedia of Dry Goods*. New York: Root Newspaper Association, 1900.

Cargo, Robert T., "Long Remembered," in *The Quilt Digest*, San Francisco, 1985.

Carter, Hodding. *The Angry Scar: The Story of Reconstruction*. New York: Doubleday, 1959.

Chattapadhyaya, Kamaladevi. Introduction to Exhibit Catalog, *India: Village Tribal Ritual Arts*. LaJolla, California: (Mingei International Museum of World Folk Art, 1981.

Coffin, Robert P. Tristram. *Collected Poems*. New York: The Macmillan Company, 1932.

Cooper, Patricia, and Norma Bradley Buford. *The Quilters: Women and Domestic Art*. Garden City, New York: Anchor Press, 1978.

Depuy, E. Ernest, and Trevor N. Depuy, *The Compact History of the Civil War*. New York: Hawthorne Books, Inc., 1960.

Duncan, Ruby Hinson, "Out of the Attic," in *Country Needlecraft*, February 1987.

Edwards, Anne. *Road to Tara: The Life of Margaret Mitchell*. New Haven and New York: Ticknor & Fields, 1983.

Finley, Ruth E. *Old Patchwork Quilts and The Women Who Made Them*. 1929. Reprint Newton Center, Massachusetts: Charles T. Branford, 1983.

Frager, Dorothy. *The Book of Sampler Quilts*. Radnor, Pennsylvania: Chilton Book Company, 1983.

Garrett, Elisabeth Donaghy, in Introduction to *Stitches in Time: A Legacy of Ozark Quilts* by Michael Luster. Rogers, Arkansas: Rogers Historical Museum, 1986.

Georgia State Gazetteer and Business Directory, 1881–82. Atlanta, Georgia. James P. Harrison & Co., 1881.

Gilbert and Bottoms Family Records, 1821–1945. Collection of Nancilu B. Burdick.

Gilbert and Bottoms records and artifacts. Collection of Ruth B. Potts.

Guffin, Robert L., Jr. *Gilbert Pioneers and Their Descendants in North Carolina and Georgia*. Tuscaloosa, Alabama: privately published, 1974.

Gutcheon, Jeffrey, "Not for Shopkeepers Only," in *Quilter's Newsletter* Magazine, No. 189, February 1987.

Hall, Carrie A., and Rose G. Kretsinger. *The Romance of the Patchwork Quilt in America.* New York: Bonanza, 1935.

Hall, Eliza Calvert. *Aunt Jane of Kentucky,* San Pedro, California: R. & E. Miles, 1986.

Harrison, Jane Ellen. *Mythology,* New York: Harcourt, Brace & World, Inc., 1963.

Heinberg, Richard, "Looking Back From the End of Time," in *Integrity International,* January–February 1987.

Hilty, Lucille. "The Passion for Quiltmaking" in *Uncoverings 1980,* Sally Garoutte, ed. Mill Valley, California: American Quilt Study Group, 1981.

History of Fayette County, 1821–1971, Carolyn C. Cary, ed. Fayetteville, Georgia: Fayette County Historical Society, 1977.

Holstein, Jonathan. *The Pieced Quilt.* Boston: Little, Brown and Company, 1973.

Irwin, John Rice. *A People and Their Quilts.* Exton, Pennsylvania: Schiffer Publishing Limited, 1963.

Jones, Margaret Jean. *Combing Cullman County.* Cullman, Alabama: Privately published, 1975.

————. *Cullman County Across the Years.* Cullman, Alabama: Privately published, 1971.

Luster, Michael. *Stitches in Time: A Legacy of Ozark Quilts.* Rogers, Arkansas: Rogers Historical Museum, 1986.

Lynch, John. Civil War scrapbook and collection of Gilbert letters and records.

Maps, Major General W. T. Sherman, compiled from captured Rebel maps by Edward Rogers, Atlanta Historical Society, Atlanta, Georgia; and Gen. Joe Wheeler, Cavalry Map of Fayette County (detail), Georgia State Archives, Atlanta, 1864.

McAdams, Robert. *Smithsonian,* January 1987.

Miller, L. D. *History of Alabama.* Birmingham, Alabama: privately published, 1901.

Naisbitt, John. *Megatrends.* New York: Warner Books, 1984.

O'Connor, Flannery. *The Complete Stories.* New York: Farrar, Straus and Giroux, 1971.

Olson, Charles. *A Special View of History.* Berkeley, California: OYEZ, 1970.

Orlofsky, Patsy and Myron. *Quilts in America.* New York: McGraw-Hill Book Company, 1974.

Potts, Ruth Butler. Collection of Talula Bottoms quilt patterns, photographs, and family documents.

Ramsey, Bets. "Design Invention in Country Quilts" in *Uncoverings 1980,* Sally Garoutte, ed. Mill Valley, California: American Quilt Study Group, 1981.

————. *Quilt Closeup: Five Southern Views.* Chattanooga, Tennessee: Hunter Museum of Art, 1983.

Rhodes, James Ford. *History of the Civil War 1861–1865.* New York, Frederick Unger Publishing Company, 1961.

Richards, Mary Caroline. *Centering in Pottery, Poetry, and the Person.* Middleton, Connecticut: Weslyan University Press, 1962.

Safford, Carleton L., and Robert Bishop. *America's Quilts and Coverlets.* New York: E. P. Dutton, 1980.

Westling, Louise. *Sacred Groves and Ravaged Gardens: The Fiction of Eudora Welty, Carson McCullers, and Flannery O'Connor.* Athens, Georgia: University of Georgia Press, 1985.

Wingate, Isabel B. *Fairchild's Dictionary of Textiles.* New York: Fairchild Publications, 1979.

Women's Day, May 1941, quoted in "Scrapbook," *Quilter's Newsletter* Magazine, December 1986.

Woolf, Virginia. *A Room of One's Own.* New York: Harcourt, Brace and World, Inc., 1929.

Index